'Congratulations to Leanne, who has produced a very insightful and practical guide to better understanding the challenges that Black women face. The book includes plenty of helpful suggestions on how we can "close the gap" by creating a supportive culture for diversity, equity, inclusion and allyship within our companies.'

Stuart White, Chief Executive Officer, HSBC Asset Management (UK) Ltd and global sponsor of its DE&I programme

'A thought-provoking and insightful narrative on the specific challenges facing Black women in the workplace. In addition to providing a window into this, Leanne helpfully delivers some potential solutions for all of us to consider.'

Gillian Hepburn, Head of Intermediary Solutions, Schroders

'Leanne Mair really hits the mark with this straight-talking analysis of the obstacles to gender equality in the workplace, seen through the eyes of Black women. An essential read for leaders and people managers, this book's direct but empathetic and practical advice is a great resource for anyone seeking to build a more equitable organization.'

Lindsey Stewart, 2021 Black British Business Awards Senior Leader Finalist, Advocate for DE&I in financial services

'*Closing the Gap* is an urgent read for allies committed to promoting gender equity beyond performative gestures. Leanne Mair offers perceptive and honest insights on workplace experiences of Black women recognisable across organizational settings. Timely and sharp, *Closing the Gap* examines both entrenched and newly emerging power dynamics highlighted by shortcomings of surface-level DEI commitments. To level the playing field for women in Western societies, Mair advocates a transformative "trickle-up" approach – moving from perceiving Black women as intruders in an unequal system to elevating Black women as evangelists of regenerative change.'

Sofia Skrypnyk, Head of Equity, Inclusion
& Human Rights, C&A

'In *Closing the Gap*, Leanne Mair highlights the intersecting and unique challenges that Black women face in the fight for gender equality. By emphasizing the importance of addressing the specific needs and experiences of Black women, Mair effectively demonstrates that achieving equality for Black women is not only crucial for their own advancement but also for the advancement of all women. This nuanced perspective encourages readers to recognize and actively participate in the dismantling of systems of oppression that disproportionately affect marginalized groups, ultimately paving the way for a more just and inclusive society for everyone.'

Kumari Williams, Vice President,
Belonging & Diversity, Workday

CLOSING THE GAP

How to include
Black Women
in any Gender Equity Strategy

Leanne Mair

BLOOMSBURY BUSINESS
LONDON · OXFORD · NEW YORK · NEW DELHI · SYDNEY

BLOOMSBURY BUSINESS
Bloomsbury Publishing Plc
50 Bedford Square, London, WC1B 3DP, UK
29 Earlsfort Terrace, Dublin 2, Ireland

BLOOMSBURY, BLOOMSBURY BUSINESS and the Diana logo are trademarks
of Bloomsbury Publishing Plc

First published in Great Britain 2023

A catalogue record for this book is available from the British Library

Library of Congress Cataloguing-in-Publication data has been applied for

ISBN: 978-1-3994-1036-6; eBook: 978-1-3994-1039-7

2 4 6 8 10 9 7 5 3 1

Typeset by Deanta Global Publishing Services, Chennai, India
Printed and bound in Great Britain by CPI Group (UK) Ltd, Croydon CR0 4YY

To find out more about our authors and books visit www.bloomsbury.com
and sign up for our newsletters

CONTENTS

Introduction

Context is everything. It forces to us to question and challenge what we see. It drives us to seek not just the bigger picture, but also the most minute detail.

And it is context that will also explain why gender equity is critical to your organization's success, why we have the corporate structures in place that we do and how this has created institutional and systemic barriers for Black women.

It is only with context that we can begin to forge meaningful solutions. Only by addressing *why* we have come to this point can we address *how* we can counteract it.

In the past two years, there has not only been a slowdown in achieving gender equality. There has been a regression. According to the UN, it is now going to take nearly 300 years to achieve gender equality whereas at the beginning of the pandemic it was 136 years. This has happened despite a heightened focus on women with NGOs, gender-lens investing and initiatives focused on women in the workplace, yet still we are stalling.

Almost all organizations today have added diversity, equity and inclusion (DEI), or environmental, social and governance (ESG), to their agenda. This has been as a result of a mixture of factors, but George Floyd's murder in May 2020 brought diversity, equity and inclusion into mainstream consciousness and has shaped and changed organizational strategy, shareholder decisions and employer relations. The by-product has been manifold: there has been a clear change in legislation, regulation and heightened expectations of organizations, most specifically in expectations of CEOs and how they respond to social injustice.

Up until this point, organizations fell into two camps: the ones that focused on the environment and the others that did not. There was seemingly no space to closely analyze the governance of organization and its impact on women but, in particular, Black women. There was a collective realization that something must be done, but less analysis on what it would entail.

The initial knee-jerk reaction of a lot of organizations has meant that action was taken, but as we move into the phase of measuring the success, outcomes and impact of this action, meaningful change seems to be markedly absent

What has driven the need for measurement?

Economic downturns have that wonderful effect of increasing budget analysis and seeing where and what the return on investment (ROI) has been and finding ways to generate economic growth. This has meant that both DEI and ESG strategies have come under the microscope like never before. Both have been paraded as ways to boost profit margins and this is now being put to the test.

Yearly budgeting, employee satisfaction surveys and leadership composition are points of reckoning. If the improvements have not been large enough, then organizations are pulling back from DEI initiatives.

How has it got to this stage?

The approach to DEI in particular has followed the standard method of focusing on key performance indicators (KPIs), quotas, percentage targets and all the other wonderful things that go into a spreadsheet in order to create SMART (Specific, Measurable, Achievable, Relevant, Time-bound) goals.

Yet in doing this they end up missing out one key element: the human aspect. Above and beyond having SMART goals, to change the landscape and culture of any organization, all goals have to have a qualitative component.

When it comes to gender equity this applies even more so, but the reality is that organizations often struggle to get to grips with gender equity, not least because there is an unwillingness to lean into the specificity that is required to accelerate it. Gender equality focuses on closing the gap between men and women, whereas gender equity demands that the hierarchy among women is dismantled.

In many cases, an apt description is that companies care about women, people within companies care, and there is a general understanding that when women win, everyone wins.

Yet this simplified vision keeps the impact narrow. Gender equality within a corporate context has further perpetuated this idealistic view, as it has avoided giving the topic deeper consideration, that reveals that women sit at many different intersections. Failure to explore these deeper issues denies companies the opportunity to achieve more in terms of gender equality.

Acknowledgement of the prevalence, variety and nuance of intersection, on the other hand, creates more meaningful and long-lasting impact.

A starting point for the examination of the intersections professional women span is disparities in earnings. The standard benchmark is a goal that women be paid and treated the same as men (specifically White men, who sit at the top of the food chain). However, the gap between what Black women, White women,

Asian women and Latina women earn is huge, and differs with geography. In America, Asian women are top earners; in Europe, White women are. Latinas in America are the lowest earners; in Europe, that position is occupied by Black women.

The idea that all women have the same opportunities and that a rising tide will lift all boats ignores the reality that feminism has not done enough specifically for Black women. This assumption that all women occupy a single grouping and are measured against White men completely misses the stratification of different groups of women.

Historically, White women have not done enough to support Black women in their fight for equality. The limits of a trickle-down effect in this space become clear when race is not included in the equation of feminism. Even as more and more White women work on issues of racism and diversity, their passion is being prioritized over the lived experiences of Black women, which is still perpetuating the same issues of mainstream feminism. The challenges that Black women face are not being centred.

White women have not been subject to the same systemic barriers that have limited the opportunities and advancement of Black women. As a result, their understanding of the issues faced by Black women is limited, and they may not fully grasp the complexities and nuances of the struggles that Black women face.

Furthermore, White women often have privilege and access to resources that Black women do not, which can make it difficult for them to truly understand the experiences and challenges they face. This makes it harder for them to develop effective solutions to the problems faced by Black women, and it can also make it harder for them to empathize with the struggles of Black women if there is no willingness to learn more about those barriers, but also to equally accept how they have benefited from the existing structure.

This has predictable results.

The voices that get heard are those with the loudest microphones, who are, by definition, not those who suffer the most deeply. This unavoidably skews a company's plan for addressing gender equality. If the group you have tasked with studying gender in your workplace is led by White women exclusively and in combination with being senior, many of the important nuances will have been lost.

Understanding the multiple layers of gender equity requires deeper exploration, and actually learning about the different issues faced by each woman in your leadership team and the broader corporate community.

A better structure for change centres on the perspective, needs and experience of Black women. Today's common trickle-down approach is not working; a 'trickle up' or 'follow up' paradigm would be more effective.

Broadening efforts and transitioning leadership focus to helping those who suffer the most will, by default, also help those who suffer to a lesser extent, because the more you address, the more you solve.

The fundamental opportunity that is missed when we focus solely, or primarily, on White women and amplify their voices to the exclusion of others is that the gaze is not as broad as it needs to be to effect change. Problems faced by women who sit at different intersections are not addressed if the view is too narrow.

We need to move beyond asking how Black women feel and instead ask them to share their lived experiences, creating opportunities to accelerate gender equity in practice. This is typically difficult in a business situation where discussion tends to revolve around a traditional set of quantifiable facts and tangible figures, which do not factor in the importance of anecdotal data, and where it is assumed that these facts and figures should be sufficient in starting on the journey to gender equity.

Movement beyond the current concept of looking at 'all women' or even 'all Black women' as a particular, standardized group takes work and causes discomfort. It is challenging to have to chart a new course, especially when the topic of racial equity is one that most people shy away from. Communication and transparency are critical to being successful in this journey.

Companies, employers and staff all need to intentionally create opportunities to talk, and to listen. You might not know what your company needs to do better, but someone in your organization does. It is probably not the person with the most powerful microphone.

Critically, this is not a moment or an excuse to place the entire burden on your Black female colleagues. It is not fair to expect them to craft the perfect three-step plan for the company to achieve gender equity in the workplace. All of that is still the job of leadership, who must shift to a position of listening and learning to do that job well. It is not acceptable to stop short, asserting that your efforts are enough. This is a process, not an event.

No one expects a company, or a person, to be perfect, but we must demand that leadership accept responsibility for listening and evolving. Clear actions are the beginning of a growth path, but must be continually followed with dialogue and improvement. Listen to your people; try to understand their experiences; accept that this is very complicated; challenge yourself to explore the multi-layered intersections and realities of gender equality. Only then can a company honestly assess its processes, policies and culture in a way that allows for meaningful change in strategy, keeping always in mind the goal of workplace equity.

It may be painful, but is not difficult, for a company to rate its own gender equality strategy. If you are not consciously incorporating intersectional analysis into your plan, it is time to change and to start on gender equity efforts.

The first step is self-assessment, but to get to this there is further context that needs to be added to how your organization currently over-leverages Black women and how you can remove those barriers.

A saying I have heard many times is 'you don't know what you don't know'. It sounds logical, yet it is probably one of the most overlooked aspects of cultural transformation. But suppose you are afraid to ask or you are concerned about burdening Black women in your organization?

There is a better way. It is this book.

Closing the Gap is a practical book that provides not only insights and case studies, but also instructions on how organizations can do the heavy lifting to ensure that they are doing everything in their power to make certain that Black women can thrive.

This book is also intended to help support some of the 104 women across Europe who completed the Experience Chasm Survey 2021.[1] The purpose of this survey was to shine a light on both the positive and negative experiences of Black women in the workplace. This was a solutions-driven survey that asked Black women what is it that they needed from their organization to be successful. What are they doing when their organization

---

[1] https://www.benefactumconsulting.com/closing-the-chasm-report

refuses to provide them with adequate support? The results were astounding. Contrary to popular belief, most of the participants were still hopeful that they could build careers and they wanted to be able to.

This signals that there is still opportunity for your organization to engage with your Black female contingent and drive change, but there was a resounding cry and the mandate for organizations is clear: BE SPECIFIC.

Under the umbrella of diversity, Black women are still being left out of the conversation. There is not focus on them, yet they are still chosen to be visible at very well selected moments, such as Black History Month or being an organizational representative, but they are not being included in decision-making that would contribute to building an equitable foundation that will ultimately increase engagement, retention and productivity.

Closing the Gap is also here to provide guidance on some of the blind spots and processes that are traditional drivers for success, yet don't have the same effect for Black women. Following the frameworks in this book will not only build awareness for gender equity, but also give insight into how it can be made a reality and implemented in daily practice.

The truth is, there is no shortcut. Equity takes investment, equity takes time, but in focusing on making evangelists of Black women within your company there's one critical key difference. Success.

The 4-Step method

I will be taking you through my 4-Step DARE – Diagnose, Assess, Recalibrate and Embed – method, which will help you to look at your processes and the mechanics of your organization through a gender equity lens and critically assess what works, what does not and where there is room for improvement.

- Diagnose: this first step will help you to articulate the problem you are trying to solve. Is the problem really that there are too few Black women in leadership or is it that you have not built a robust pipeline? Both could be a result of lack of opportunities given to Black women, but finding the root cause will determine the effective starting point. A lack of Black women in leadership may mean that there is an issue in the promotion process, which may need to be closely analyzed, versus not having a pool of Black female talent, the source of which could be that Black women have started working at the company and then left. Why have they left? Or, alternatively, why aren't they applying?
- Assess: this second step will help to look at the processes, people and procedures that are supporting this issue. This might be a Human Resources manager who requires training on the need to overhaul the promotion criteria because it is skewed against Black women.
- Recalibrate: this step is where things start to get uncomfortable because the conversations are no longer theoretical, but now require action: organizing the training sessions and announcing a new promotion process business-wide.
- Embed: this is another dynamic step that requires tweaking. It is the measurement part of the process. Are all the changes working and, if not, what can be optimized? What changes, both positive and negative, have we seen, and is there a way to actively measure them?

These four steps will support your organization by removing the need for Black women to do all the heavy lifting.

Bear in mind that Black women have historically had the worst experience in the workplace, but have also been disproportionately impacted by the COVID-19 pandemic as well as by the subsequent economic turbulence. The role of the employer in driving gender equity thus becomes even more important. The pandemic has led to more Black women feeling more comfortable working from home to avoid racism in the workplace, but also to the stagnation in their careers due to the 'Zoom Ceiling'. Creating a culture that engenders inclusion and belonging will be the defining characteristic of any organization that is future forward and wants to be successful.

How can you create a workplace and culture that fosters inclusion and belonging, ensuring that Black women have the chance to thrive, without putting the burden on them to drive the solutions and action?

Good governance is the answer: it is the main driver of building sustainable, long-lasting and impactful process, which will also be accelerated when you have the buy-in and sign-off of Black women within your organization.

How can you achieve this?

First, by deconstructing the corporate system.

We have to understand the barriers of the corporate system and who put them in place. When did they start? Why is there resistance to change? Only then is it possible to understand how deep-seated the issues and how strong the foundations are that slow down Black women's success, to then rebuild your relationship with Black women in your company; because, fundamentally, while White women are making significant progress, this isn't trickling down to Black women at the same speed.

The current system means that many Black women begin to question themselves and start to believe that they must be doing something wrong, especially as they see other women progressing more quickly and this is constantly validating, either explicitly or implicitly, the idea that Black women are the problem. It is not true, but without unpicking the topic it becomes easy to think that Black women are at fault.

I went through the same experience believing that I was the problem, but at the point where I started to build a network of Black women who were also professionals I understood two critical things. One: there was commonality in our experience in the treatment we received; and, two, that most of the organizations haven't been interested in learning about what Black women think, feel or need in order to progress, and what their journey is like. For the most part, we've been swept under the carpet. We've been ignored. Up until that fateful day in May 2020, when George Floyd was murdered, Black women became visible, but only visible, not valued, not recognized. But visible.

The difference between performative reactions and genuine ones has been telling, especially as organizations were under pressure to show that Black women had a value in their company. Many of the responses were revealing, as there was a clear divergence on the action taken and the impact on Black women in their organizations.

There were organizations crying out for Black women, and although many have become heads of DEI or are becoming heads of DEI committees, it is clear that Black women are still feeling exhausted and excluded within their workplaces.

Despite what feels like their best efforts, so many organizations are at a loss as to why they are still struggling to engage and retain Black women; however, they are hesitant, almost reluctant, to take the necessary steps to specifically address what is clearly a cultural and governance issue on their side.

Historically, women didn't have a place within the working structure. Black women particularly were hired out of sheer desperation because there was no longer any manpower. And there also weren't enough White women to work, so from the outset, Black women haven't been welcomed into the workforce with open arms.

Their voices weren't seen as necessary to progress or to grow; they were reduced to a mere function. Not only that, they weren't and even today aren't seen as ideal consumers. So when looking at the whole sales cycle of creating a product, building the workforce to create the product, creating ideas, launching the product in the market and building a loyal customer base, Black women have been largely overlooked.

What it also means is that within the workplace there is an inherent systemic devaluing of the Black female voice, which means that applying a gender equity lens will involve closely analyzing the power structure and hierarchy.

It isn't about closing the gap between Black women and White men, but closing the gap in this hierarchy among women.

So let's begin there ...

CHAPTER ONE

The Context

As uncomfortable as it is to read, the hierarchy within society and especially within the corporate setting is clear, but for emphasis, here is what I call the power pyramid.

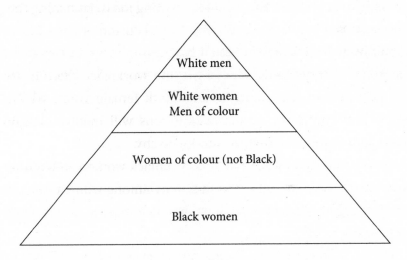

The impact of the power pyramid

The power pyramid also dictates how the interests, needs and wants of each group are considered, and indeed, whether they are considered at all. The direct impact is that the interests, needs and wants of Black women have always been seen as a luxury and not a necessity to the success of any business.

Gender equality has traditionally been focused on achieving parity between White women and White men, with the assumption that elevating the status of White women will automatically lead to equality for all women. However, this approach has not been effective in addressing the needs and experiences of Black women, who are often marginalized within both the feminist movement and society as a whole.

This hierarchy is maintained through systemic barriers and discrimination, and it has been difficult to break down. This means that even when progress is made in elevating the status of White women this does not necessarily lead to true equity for Black women.

Subliminally, the way in which Black women are often viewed and treated in the workplace can perpetuate the idea that they are not fully human, but, rather, a function of the organization. This way of thinking is rooted in the history of racial discrimination and exploitation, and it is both harmful and outdated.

Think back to the time when all women were property rather than people. This was only changed, depending on the location, in the early 1900s. Prior to that, a woman belonged to her husband or her father.

Yet for a Black woman, being a person with her own rights, being able to make decisions independently of a man and also entering the workforce independently of a man occurred far later. This wave effect of White women taking priority, although Black women also fought on their behalf, is still perpetuated in the workplace today and is the reason why *Closing the Gap* is so vitally important.

Even the entry of Black women into the workplace was under duress. It was only with the onset of the First World War that Black women (in the US) were invited to join the workforce, not because they were wanted but because there was simply no other choice.

But as soon as possible, they were forced out of the workforce once again, into jobs that were considered menial in comparison to the work they had done during the war. For the longest time, the only work that could be accessed for Black women was taking care of families, cleaning and working in factories.

The type of work in and of itself confirmed subliminally that this was all Black women were good at doing. Although they were often nannies, which meant they were running households and educating children, they were never seen as intelligent, capable or sometimes even human, which reflects many of the systemic issues of racism and sexism within the workplace that upholds these very stereotypes.

Here are some questions for you to consider:

- How could your organization be implicitly or subliminally upholding stereotypes?

Tip: look at the positions in your organization where there is a high concentration of Black women. Are they in budget-holding and/or client-facing positions or are they in the background and only present for DEI committee work?

- Do you seem to be suffering from the 'broken rung' phenomenon?

Tip: what is the root cause? Is it due to Black women leaving an organization and high turnover at a junior level, or is there an organizational issue that hasn't been delved into more deeply?

One of the main keys to success when it comes to gender equity is prioritizing the interests, needs and wants of the group of women you are trying to empower, in this case Black women. The dangers of not doing this are that you risk not only doing more damage on an individual basis, but also on a collective one – by further entrenching Black women as stereotypes, organizations create and affirms the already existing belief system that they cannot grow, they cannot innovate and they cannot lead, which could not be further from the truth.

We have been conditioned to think about gender equality in very narrow terms. Race has been viewed as a secondary factor so that the intersection of gender and race has been ignored, relegated to an issue that comes later. For men, it can often feel too difficult and uncomfortable to counter. Gender equality is still a phrase that many hide behind to claim that they are fighting for all women when the truth is that women are being considered within one lens only, which is usually to the benefit of White women.

This is why gender equity is so important: it acknowledges a critical difference. That equitable treatment will not look the same but examines all the factors that disadvantage each group from a systemic and institutional perspective. Yet, most importantly, it is also about leaning into the discomfort of embracing the work needed for gender equity. If inclusion and belonging are the goal of every organization, then wanting to make evangelists of Black women within should be prioritized over any personal or organizational discomfort.

The other negative effect of the power pyramid is that the Black female corporate footprint has been deemed too small to invest in or to care about in a meaningful way, so while a lot of organizations are happy to have the faces of the Black female employees front and centre on every piece of promotional literature going, they are still not fully committing to making the necessary internal changes.

Diversity has become another word to hide behind to prove that there are plans in the pipeline, but the missing link is that there is very little listening to and learning about what can be done better and what meaningful support could look like.

When I think about all the organizations that exist around supporting Black women, whether it's an association within the legal industry, asset management or financial services, architecture or marketing, the agenda is clear. The fact that these associations exist tells us that these industries are not doing what they should and are not doing more than committing to providing support.

One of the most frequent questions I get asked is: 'If I don't have the data about how many Black women are in my organization, how can I do anything to help them?' This is a valid question, but it is also one for which a shift in perspective is required.

Focusing on a number means that you are no longer focused on the impact, even if it is only one Black woman. Her power is not only being an employee; her power is in her network and what she will say about her employer, about how she will advise others to interact, or not, with the brand, but also her potential to help you get this right. Not because she will build you a plan and help you execute it, but because you will be including her feedback as part of your strategy.

The mistake a lot of organizations are continuing to make in this climate, where inclusion is the focus, is that they are still using the Black woman as a function. She becomes a face or a tool that can placate a shareholder audience and a consumer audience, but, interestingly, never an employee audience, as the focus for most organizations is heavily external.

Although this is rarely so explicitly articulated in meetings, the feeling a lot of Black women have is that their employers have said: 'How can we keep selling our services and products without making any changes to our business, while still giving the impression that we're making changes to our business?'

This is usually what leads to the disenfranchisement of the female Black community within your organization, but it also drives a wedge within the group.

How?

Focusing on the external rather than internal means that there is a 'chosen one'. She is the ultimate brand evangelist, she is the one chosen for panels, corporate photos, commentary in the news and she is not to be criticized because she is doing this to accelerate change (we will look at this exploitation further later on in the book), but for the other Black women in the organization it seems hypocritical because they are not seeing any changes in their daily lives.

This mechanism of having a 'chosen one' allows too many to circumvent the discomfort of doing the work, but there are no shortcuts or diversions for sustainable and meaningful change.

Going back to the power of Black women within an organization, they have every organizations' reputation in the palm of their hand and it will be in these unofficial networks and associations that the truth will come out.

Throughout the past two years we've seen a lot of companies articulate their commitments to the Black female economy externally, whether it's through investing in Black female businesses, doing things on the ground with grassroots associations or looking at the impact of climate change; but what we're also seeing on the other side is that large groups of Black women are leaving these companies. Or, even worse, they're staying but they're disengaged. They're no longer willing to be the face. They're no longer willing to fight for their positions. Because they've been beaten down by a company that is being praised externally for all its good work and has come to believe that this external praise somehow correlates with making progress or doing right by Black women.

This book isn't about calling out every single organization for what they're not doing, but we have to look honestly at where we are today and how we got there. The purpose of this book is really to outline that, without gender equity and without creating systemic changes, in five years from now we won't have seen any more progress but, rather, a regression. With Black women being the largest demographic leaving the corporate world to start their own businesses, now is the time to focus on retention.

With increased regulation and an increased focus on what's being done within a company, being unaware or unsure will not be an acceptable excuse. It will have been a deliberate decision. What we can't have five years from now is companies that still have all-White boards even if the composition of the board is 20, 30 or 50 per cent female. It is not reflective of where the talent is. The question this book answers is how individuals and organizations can commit to gender equity and what contributes and detracts from it. How can you upskill your gender equality efforts into gender equity practice?

To understand this, there are several things we have to look at: how women are placed within organizations and what are the hidden issues that are faced within the company, whether it's from a governance perspective or a cultural perspective, that result in Black women being held back.

How can companies not just meet them halfway, but rather go over and above in order not only to close this chasm but also to put systems and ideas, processes and procedures in place to ensure that the women within their company get what they need in order to progress? Because this book is about making evangelists of existing employees, we won't be looking at recruitment processes, but instead at the intricacies and nuances of being a Black woman within the workplace, what works and what doesn't, and the issues that can and should be eradicated, improved or refined.

It is often said that the workplace reflects society, and this is why understanding the historical and societal context is crucial when examining the interactions between employers and Black female employees. The way Black women are treated in the workplace is not an isolated phenomenon, but a reflection of the broader societal issues of racism and discrimination that Black women have historically faced and continue to face today.

In order to fully understand and address the challenges faced by Black women in the workplace, it is important to examine the ways in which they have been historically marginalized and discriminated against in society. For example, in the US, Black women have faced a long history of discrimination, starting with the exploitation of their labour during slavery, and continuing through the Jim Crow laws and the modern-day pay gap.

Societal discrimination has also limited Black women's access to education and job opportunities, and created a system in which they are disproportionately represented in low-paying jobs, with limited opportunities for advancement. This, in turn, has affected how Black women are treated in the workplace, where they are often subject to discrimination and bias and face barriers to advancement and success.

The power pyramid that exists in society has a significant impact not only on the workplace, but also on how different groups of people are perceived and treated. One of the main forms of stereotyping that Black women face is the issue of visibility versus scrutiny or, in many cases, invisibility.

Black women are often invisible in the workplace, where they are under-represented in leadership roles and face barriers to promotion and advancement. This invisibility can also extend to societal perceptions, where Black women are sometimes not seen as fully human, but, rather, as a stereotype or a function of the organization.

On the other hand, when Black women are visible, they often face intense scrutiny and criticism, where they are held to a higher standard than others and are not given the same empathy and support. This scrutiny can also manifest itself in microaggressions and discrimination, which can create a hostile and unwelcoming environment in the workplace.

The power pyramid also plays a role in the way that Black women are represented in the media, where they are often depicted in a stereotypical and negative light, and their experiences and perspectives are not fully represented. This lack of representation and visibility in the media can further contribute to societal perceptions of Black women and reinforce the idea that they are invisible or only valuable for their diversity.

The same trend of invisibility and lack of representation that Black women face in the workplace and in society is also reflected in the way their historical footprint is viewed and remembered. In many European countries, there is an unwillingness to fully engage with their own history as it pertains to slavery, particularly when it comes to the Black female footprint.

In addition, too, there is a lack of acknowledgement and recognition of the role that European people's ancestors played in the transatlantic slave trade and the atrocities that were committed against enslaved people. This failure of acknowledgement and recognition is reflected in the lack of representation of Black female historical figures in national narratives and public monuments, which perpetuates the idea that their contributions and experiences are not important or worth remembering.

This lack of engagement with their own history, understanding of the legacy of slavery and the ongoing effects of discrimination has perpetuated the marginalization of Black women in European societies today, not least in the workplace.

There is, however, a difference in approach across Europe. In Germany, for example, the issue of marginalization is still very much under the radar due to historical issues around collecting census data, although sprouts are beginning to shoot that challenge this. In France, the conversation is slightly different because you're French first and any other nationality thereafter. In Britain, the nuance of the Black experience has been engulfed into the categorization of BAME (Black, Asian, Minority, Ethnic) and/or women of colour. There is a general reticence about engaging with the topic and certainly not in the context of a positive contribution or having been innovators and leaders. It is only really within the context of the US explicitly that the footprint has been heat-mapped, if you will.

It has been discussed ad infinitum because historically the relationship that the US has with Black women has been documented. Whether entwined with trauma or not, it is still there to be found if you go and look for it. From the point of slavery to the point of today, there is a clear thread of acknowledging the existence of the Black female footprint, acknowledging the existence of Black women and their contribution, although their true value has not been recognized.

By not recounting the truth, the narratives and stereotypes that have been built so far cannot be challenged and Black women are still being positioned as 'less than' or incapable. This is where there is a marked difference when comparing the US to Europe because Europe has, for the most part, ignored the footprint of Black women.

If we take, in the UK, what became known as the Windrush generation as one example, here, some of the Black women who were invited from the West Indies worked as nurses and midwives in the 1950s and radically changed the hygiene standards of the NHS. This narrative has been overlooked and ignored. The improvements to medical hygiene standards have continued to save lives to this day yet their contribution and impact is scarcely spoken of.

At the height of the COVID-19 pandemic in the UK, it was Black women who were dying in disproportionate numbers. Why? Because they were on the front line as nurses, as midwives, as carers in residential homes, yet were still being treated as a mere function and not as human beings. Ultimately, the role that Black women have played in building the British economy, working in so many different industries, has allowed modern-day Britain to become what it has.

Black women are now demanding acknowledgement, payment and recognition for work that they have done in the past and continue to do today. The legacy of our contributions has been kept within the Black communities, but not within wider society, which is why there is discomfort when Black women are asking for their dues.

We have to develop the language to speak specifically, as the contributions from the beginning of time by Black women have blurred into the background and merged into focusing on the outcomes. This can be seen in the feminist movement: everyone knows about Gloria Steinem, and her contribution is famous, but Dorothy Pitman Hughes, who was in that celebrated *Esquire* photograph of 1971 with Steinem, has not received the same acclaim, nor has her work received the same recognition. This extends to the mainstream adoption of the #MeToo movement, where Tarana Burke can still remain unseen by many audiences even though she was the originator.

When it comes to Black women being involved, we have been taught to focus on the result rather than to attribute success correctly. We fail to acknowledge that Black women are at the forefront of change, strategizing as well as protesting for all marginalized and minoritized groups, yet their contribution is still seen as being negligible because the true extent hasn't been discussed.

This is what we are also failing to do when it comes to the Black female footprint. We're looking at it in terms of absolute percentages, not in terms of what Black women's contribution is. A lot of rhetoric in the UK or in Europe around Black women is that there isn't enough qualified talent, but the question is: who is setting the standards and determining what 'qualified' means?

The top of the hierarchy determines who is qualified, who fits and what professionalism is. Then there is the added layer of context and nuance to this when you are in a country where you are minoritized or marginalized and you do not have the same foundations, generational wealth and inheritance possibilities as those whose history and foundations have been in that country for centuries.

This means that in the context of the workplace or the corporate space that doesn't acknowledge Black women, not only are Black women conditioned to work twice as hard to get half as much, but the workplace *expects* them to work twice as hard for half as much.

There is still not enough recognition of what Black women bring to the table and the level of impact they have, and because they're also not trained to shout about how much they have accomplished for fear of being targeted, there are still several gaps in the workplace culture that need to be closed.

Getting to this point involves a combination of both structural and systemic issues that still need to be addressed, and will be addressed in this book. After reading it, I want you to feel empowered to be able to create an environment where Black women feel proud of being able to name their accomplishments without it being within the context of diversity, equity and inclusion, without it being tokenistic in order to validate that the company they work for is equitable; but, rather, as an acknowledgement of their dedication, ambition, determination and success in delivering not just what they've been asked to deliver, but above and beyond.

It is important to note that data alone cannot fully capture the experiences and perspectives of Black women in the workplace. While data can provide valuable insights and information, it is often limited in its ability to fully convey the complex and intersecting issues that Black women face. Additionally, data can often reinforce existing biases and stereotypes, and does not always accurately reflect the lived experiences of Black women.

Furthermore, data can also be used to justify the lack of progress or action on issues of equity, by focusing on the lack of representation of Black women in leadership positions or other areas of the company rather than addressing the root causes of these disparities.

Parts of gender equality promote the concept of women having it all – being a career woman and a mother as the aim we should all have – but what it fails to encompass is that this has long been the reality for a lot of Black women, not out of choice, both historically and today.

A lot of Black women have had no choice but to work while having children without the acknowledgement of their struggle and without the allowances, conversation and support that have been introduced within recent years for White women explicitly.

This is not to say that all women are mothers, but it does add a nuance that informs how some Black women are allowed to show up in the corporate space. Black female humanity has been erased in the corporate space, which in turn reduces the space for vulnerability and emotions. Accelerating gender equity requires understanding the context of the Black female footprint, and that includes understanding the Black woman's journey.

Women can frequently be positioned as intruders within the workplace, and the detrimental effect of this is compounded for Black women. Yet creating discourse around this topic should not be seen as being divisive, but as a start to discovering both convergences and divergences in experience.

It is in embracing those divergences that there is a chance of finding long-lasting solutions. We have to be willing to acknowledge and embrace the existence of Black women within the workplace in the truest sense.

This means recognizing and valuing their unique experiences and perspectives, rather than treating them as a monolithic group or expecting them to conform to the dominant culture. It also means actively working to dismantle the systemic barriers and biases that prevent Black women from thriving in the workplace.

To encapsulate Black women's experience in the workplace, we must always start with recognition of the assumptions in play. Black women never have the opportunity to make a first impression. They are always (pre)judged within a context of common assumptions as well as the personal experience of those they meet at work.

When she first presents herself, whether to an interviewer, hiring manager, or new colleagues, a Black woman is automatically compared to other Black women those people know. There is no blank slate upon which she can convey her own abilities, talents and personality. There is already a score on the board. If she meets people who have never known or worked with other Black women, a collection of common assumptions forms the benchmark instead.

The questions she will likely be expected to answer, and the reactions with which she is met, are founded on these (and other) assumptions:

- there is one, monolithic Black culture, as defined by the media, headlines and data analysts without nuance, insight, or open minds;
- Black women lack support, especially towards educational achievement;
- linguistic comparisons are made (referred to as Ebonics in the US and considered a language in its own right as opposed to a dialect or

vernacular, and presumed to indicate ignorance or, at the very least, otherness);

- nearly every Black person grew up in a single-parent family;
- if a Black family has money, the source must be dubious or perhaps even criminal;
- Black women are hypersexual and dress provocatively for attention.

Too often these negative (and obviously untrue) assumptions form the basis of determinations on how an individual Black woman will perform within the workplace. Even people who have an intellectual understanding that one's history, skin colour and gender are not predictive of future professional performance often unconsciously rely upon assumptions as an indication, or even a guide, to what and who Black women are. These are the people who refuse to understand that referring to a Black woman as 'articulate' isn't necessarily a compliment. Why must a Black woman graciously accept this 'compliment' that is based upon an assumption that she is less than others, and that speaking well in one's first language is some kind of victory over her natural self?

The one thing we do know wholly and completely about assumptions is that they damage our capacity to learn. Assumptions allow us to revert to stereotypes in order to make a judgement. Even when a bias is unconscious (or partially so), assumptions are deliberate decisions that people make based on what they presume to be facts. And these assumptions feed into interactions, and form the basis upon which people make decisions.

When we look back on the list of common assumptions above, it is clear that in concert they form a very powerful picture of what people expect of Black women and the benchmarks against which they are judged. That picture is, in almost all cases, very far from reality. Because Black women are systematically judged on an entirely different scale from their White counterparts, they automatically feel isolated in the workplace. They never quite belong because in turning up as their genuine selves they are judged based on the assumptions of others.

Human Resources managers often cannot understand the basis of this sense of isolation because they themselves hold the same set of assumptions that exacerbate the divide. Their job is to create and follow processes and procedures that are based on these assumptions. The processes, in turn, create and reward behaviours based on flawed assumptions, and so the cycle continues. And since a sense of isolation felt by Black women at work can't really be quantified, Human Resources people can't (or won't) deal with it.

All this is why it is past time to make the effects of these assumptions tangible. Now is the time to show the world exactly what this means and the effects of the current tapestry of assumptions. It is time to push for organizations to understand that tweaking processes and procedures will not create substantive change without shifting mindsets and behaviours to ensure that Black women are seen, heard and valued.

However, in order to better understand how organizations can do this, we need to further explore the impact of women being positioned as 'the intruder'.

CHAPTER TWO

The Intruder

Usually, when we think about the word 'intruder', the first images that spring to mind are in a criminal context. The definition of 'intruder', according to the *Collins Dictionary*, is a person who goes into a place where they're not supposed to be; the essential meaning is someone who does not belong.

While it is not explicitly stated, women, and particularly Black women, are often positioned as intruders in the workplace. Despite the increasing number of female CEOs and other women in leadership positions, the conversations around women in the workplace often reveal a lack of parity in experience. Women, especially Black women, are still facing discrimination and bias in the workplace, which creates barriers to promotion, advancement and success.

Men are not picketing outside the office and saying 'Send women back home!' or 'They don't belong here!'. But that's because they don't have to. The sentiment is reinforced and embedded in all the structures. Legislation. Corporate governance that drives a company. It's reinforced by the conversations that we have around maternity leave and the slow changes to accommodate parental leave, by the conversations we have around dress codes, where the nature of being professional is the attempt to adapt the code of a man wearing a suit and creating a women's version.

It's the fact that women have been inherently paid less from their point of entry into the workforce. It's the fact that we're still fighting the gender pay gap, and being forced to justify why women should be paid the same. It's the same reason that we still have to highlight that there are different leadership styles, not just the traditional way that we've seen over and over again, which has led to the existing structures with White men dominating these positions in most corporations. The fight is still on to create space for women at the top and the trade-off is that most of the women who make it to the top are still having to jump through hoops and shed some of their authenticity to get their seat at the table.

The corporate rules have been defined by men for men, and the resistance to a complete overhaul is strong. There is no part of being a woman in the workplace that means you are completely welcome. And success is predicated on being able to follow these rules and live up to the standards imposed by the rules, which were never created with women in mind.

The difference is often seen in women-led businesses, where personal experience can drive equitable processes; however, this still does not mean that there is racial equity. A historical hierarchy has been created among women within Western society, and still exists there – and in the workplace – today. The historical interactions between Black and White women meant that, within the US context, White women ran the household with Black women doing the domestic work. Within the UK context, Black women were invited to do the jobs that were not wanted by the British. This established the tone of relations between both groups, but when all groups of women were needed to work, it created a new world.

The power pyramid and pay gaps

When we think about the gender pay gap, it seems unimaginable that women receive less money because of their race, but this is exactly how the gaps started and were subsequently used to reinforce the hierarchy.

Black women were deliberately paid less from the outset, an imbalance that was connected to their so-called lack of intellectual capacity. It is bad enough that the contribution of women is viewed as having less value than men's, but that there is also a value hierarchy among women further compounds the narrative of less-than.

This underscores the importance of closing the pay gap among women, too. Until we flatten this damaging hierarchy, it still positions the contribution of Black women as not having the same weight as White women.

Initiatives such as gender pay gap reporting and ethnicity pay gap reporting are not the whole solution, but they are strong signals to show commitment in admitting that there is a hierarchical problem that organizations are not only willing to face, but also to change.

Pay gaps are an implicit affirmation because we have been conditioned to avoid talking about pay and gaslit ('gaslighting' is a term originating from the 1944 film *Gaslight*, where a person or group causes someone to doubt their own perception of reality) into thinking it is uncouth to have these conversations, but transparency is one of the critical pillars for an organization to embed change – being truthful about where you are, where you would like to be and the difficulties in achieving these goals.

There are also the explicit ways that the positioning of being an intruder manifests itself within an organization, and this can be seen in processes where support is required.

For example, incidences of harassment can have a significant impact on Black women in the workplace, not only because of the harassment itself, but also because of the way they are treated in response to it. Black women may be less likely to report harassment due to fear of retaliation, and when they do report it they may be met with disbelief, minimization or blame. This can result in feelings of isolation, trauma and mistrust in the workplace, which can ultimately lead to the end of their careers.

In many cases, the incidents are not taken on the basis of the victim's account. Instead, the matter becomes a question of the victim's credibility and – if the accused happens to be a senior White man – a battle of endorsements and character references.

Returning to the concept of Black women being seen as functions of a business rather than human beings, finding themselves unable to openly vocalize how they feel or being faced with interrogation often leaves them with limited options, or none at all, in being able to navigate these types of situations and still keep their jobs.

Being viewed as an intruder also means that when something bad happens there is usually one option and that is for the person to leave their job, in many cases without a severance package. In those situations where there are packages, it comes with an NDA (non-disclosure agreement), which can make it difficult for the person to find new employment, as they are unable to speak about their experiences at the previous organization. This further perpetuates the cycle of discrimination and harassment in the workplace, as perpetrators are not held accountable for their actions and are able to continue to harm other employees. It also makes it difficult for the organization to truly address the issue and make necessary changes, as the voices and experiences of the victims are silenced. This is why it is so important for organizations to have clear and effective mechanisms in place for reporting and addressing incidents of harassment and discrimination.

Being seen and treated as a function also means that even though Black women are sometimes given their dues, their ability to be accepted and seen is still only linked to what they deliver to the business. Even when they are recognized, they are not afforded the privilege of showing up and being appreciated as themselves.

The ability to show up as yourself is directly correlative to productivity, and this is how organizations can win. Creating a culture where Black women are not forced to self-validate and continuously have to prove that they are worth being valued is crucial for organizations to retain and support the success of their Black female employees. This can involve actively listening to and addressing the experiences and concerns of Black women, providing opportunities for career development and advancement, and fostering a culture of inclusion and belonging. Additionally, it's important to recognize that creating a culture where Black women can show up as themselves is not only beneficial for the individual employees, but also for the organization as a whole, as it can lead to increased productivity, creativity and innovation.

How can organizations avoid the mechanisms that continue to position Black women as intruders? What are the drivers that restrict Black women from becoming evangelists? How can organizations recognize the blind spots that prevent progress? How can organizations ensure that they are doing enough, so that Black women are not required to do the heavy lifting, becoming the accelerators of change?

Admitting that corporate rules have been created through a racist and sexist lens is an important step in recognizing the systemic barriers that Black women face in the workplace. This acknowledgement is necessary for creating a culture where Black women are valued and treated as full members of the organization, rather than as intruders. By acknowledging the ways in which the corporate rules have been shaped by racism and sexism, organizations can begin to dismantle these barriers and create a more inclusive and equitable workplace.

This positioning demands that Black women constantly have to defend and prove their intelligence, consciously choose their words and actions, when expressing their feelings, being mindful of the way their appearance and speech may be perceived by others, all while trying to succeed in a system that was never created to welcome them.

There are initiatives such as the CROWN Act and the Halo Code in the US and UK, respectively, that seek to dismantle hair discrimination within the workplace as a way to combat the implicit and explicit hostility faced by Black women there. Hair should not be a topic, but for Black women, the need to assimilate and to be aligned with the dress codes and professionalism has led to their being forced to change their appearance in order to fit in and succeed.

An organization that remains open to talking but is unwilling to change is still a hostile environment. Gender equity takes action in order to promote, advance and accelerate the success of Black women within organizations. There can be no bifurcation of gender and race or postponement until later. There is no gender equality without gender equity.

This book is here to highlight blind spots and give insight, to provide advice. If you're an HR manager, can you see this happening in front of your face? Are you somebody who's looking and thinking about why your organization is losing Black women at a rate of knots or is not engaged with them? Why aren't they progressing in the organization? What is the source of their dissatisfaction?

The answer is that a lot of it lies in the company's culture processes. This book also explores how Black women are being exploited through their desire to see change and be part of that change to make a better company. It is also due to them being forced to navigate a workplace that is heavily skewed against them. Another cause is the lack of both physical and psychological security, but also the fact that they extend themselves only to be disappointed because the changes that they have worked for are not coming to fruition.

And, ultimately, the true reason that Black women are viewed as intruders, and all women in general, is because we were never supposed to be in the workplace.

When we are faced with behaviours that confirm this intruder belief, as expressed by racism or sexism, the discomfort pushes us to rely on the concept of unconscious bias, even though to all intents and purposes that is a lazy excuse. We have been socialized to believe in the truth of the hierarchy, but concepts such as unconscious bias create space to remove blame. It upholds the belief that ensures that this behaviour is seen as being passive when in many instances it is actually deliberate.

A Black woman's point of entry to being made to feel like an intruder can begin at the application or interview stages – for example, if she chooses not to use an anglicized name – and follows her all the way through to sitting in the C-suite and having the extra burden of being showcased as the high-achieving 'superwoman', the exception to the rule and an example to those who should just be 'more dedicated'.

When it comes down to really deconstructing the premise of organization, its origins and the culture that has been created, with the backdrop of women being an intruder, there is a clear path as to why not all women get to show up authentically and why the paths to success look drastically different. It sheds a light on how the gender pay gap remains an agenda point, but is not taken seriously.

Society also needs to legislate more to ensure that women are supported in being welcomed in the workplace. If society and organizations do not actively fight against the intruder perception, they inherently support the belief that Black women should be in positions of servitude. And the expectation in many organizations today is that Black women know their place and still maintain some of these servile behaviours. Stereotypes such as 'the angry Black woman' or 'the difficult colleague' have been created to keep Black women in check, and as they push more to be seen and heard, the intrusion seems louder than ever.

When they fail to acknowledge the intrusion principle, the unintended consequence is that companies place themselves in conflicting positions. On the one hand they focus on increasing female presence in leadership, but on the other they do not critically question why more Black women are not making it through and assess their process to see what barriers they are creating. By not being proactive enough with change, they are implying that Black women who do make it through to leadership positions are 'shooting above their station'.

Now, it is possible that this hasn't been articulated in this way before, as we are used to Black women being positioned as the ones who are responsible for the deficits – the usual excuses being 'we can't find suitable Black women for this role', 'we cannot find anyone with the right qualifications', or 'they just don't apply here'.

The responsibility sits firmly with organizations to do more, but what is not acknowledged is that they are what I call giving themselves 'permission to be passive'. They imply that it is Black women's fault that they're not within their organization when, in reality, this is just as much an excuse to avoid engaging with discomfort. Permission to be passive transfers responsibility and gives grace to those who are unwilling to do anything different, but expect different results. They are not willing to accept that the standards they have set are based upon gender- and race-related exclusivity.

As early as the 1880s, job descriptions that appeared were very clear about which jobs were for men and which were for women. Interestingly, the requirements were less about what the job entailed and more about personal prerequisites, such as nurses being expected to be single or widowed, and prepared 'to make themselves generally and genuinely useful'. Another job description from the US in 1887 for a nurse states that any nurse 'who smokes, uses liquor in any form, gets her hair done at a beauty shop or frequents dancehalls will give the director of nurses good reason to suspect her worth, intentions and integrity'. From the very beginning, the determining factors for women were less about their ability to deliver, but formed by what a 'good woman' was according to men. These were the hoops that had to be jumped through in order to have a certain amount of freedom.

Creating equitable workplaces is about removing these hoops that are only applicable for some, and until those gender-specific and race-specific hoops are gone we will still have a workplace optimized for White male success.

With two world wars, a lack of male staff and industrialization, we reached the point where women were needed to do jobs that men had previously done, but there were still clear lines of demarcation between masculine and feminine jobs. Slowly came the development of secretarial pools and PA training, and while there were a few Black women in the workforce, there was no critical mass to develop a huge footprint.

Previously, recruitment was mostly conducted from a pool of candidates who were similar in terms of race, gender and ethnicity to the business owners, and the main requirements were the right skill set and the willingness to work. However, as many businesses owned by Black families began to expand and the demographic of the British population began to change, and Black communities created more and more opportunities for their children, it meant that Black people were pushing into the corporate space without waiting for an invitation. It was always going to be seen as an intrusion.

Now, the requirements for fitting into a business or organization are carefully defined and prescriptive. To be a good cultural fit, you need the right education, hobbies and connections. Looking back at the power pyramid, Black women have the least in common with those who are at the top, so they have to do more to be able to fit into this exclusive club and to create less resistance towards their intrusion. The stereotypes that Black women face within the workplace are in many ways designed to keep them in their place and to continuously remind them of this intrusion; that they aren't supposed to be there, but rather that they have been benevolently allowed to inhabit this space. And that their behaviour, when it is called out, is a regression to who they really are.

The concept of the intrusion also disproves the theory that progress within organizations is based on meritocracy alone. If those who are the most qualified are progressing at the slowest rate, it shows that there are systemic rather than personal issues, especially when assimilation and the need to fit in are also included. Context changes the outcome and this is why it is so important that you are here now, reading this chapter. Without this context and searching for gender equity as well as gender equality, there is no chance of achieving true diversity, equity and inclusion in your culture.

Acting without context is like trying to reach a destination without a form of navigation. To avoid movement without progress means coming to terms with the power structure and where Black women sit within this hierarchy.

Social media is peppered with questions about Black women, such as 'Why do they feel oppressed?' or 'How bad or different can it be to be a Black woman in the workplace?' When looked at within the context of an intrusion, an intruder is on the receiving end of aggressive or distasteful behaviour, so the burden that Black women are carrying is that they are often faced with colleagues who make it clear that they would prefer them to be somewhere else. Not only that, but being on the receiving end of this treatment means that they are forced to be defensive and aware to ensure that they survive in this environment. The role of your organization's processes and culture is to ensure that they thrive, not just survive.

Let's take the McKinsey and LeanIn.org Women in the Workplace reports of 2019 and 2021,[1] which showed that there have been improvements for White women in the workplace, but for Black women and other women of colour there have been no improvements. This reinforces the fact that gender equality is still not actively working for the benefit of all women. The welcome is not being extended across the board, and the hierarchy is still very much in force.

So, the question for most companies is: firstly, are you willing to accept that women are seen as an intrusion? And secondly, are you willing to accept that the journey for Black women is vastly different?

Answering yes to both questions puts you at the start of this path to understanding more about gender equity and how you and your organization can do more for Black women. The aim is to extend a welcome through making changes in governance that will drive cultural change.

It is often forgotten that the employer/employee relationship is a mutually beneficial one. I like to think of it as a host and a guest but the difference here is that the guest is also bringing and cooking the food and the host is paying for it. Both make

---

[1] https://leanin.org/women-in-the-workplace/2021/women-of-color-continue-to-have-a-worse-experience-at-work

a contribution that creates a great dinner, but we often focus on how much more employees need to do for their employers, when there is a lot more that organizations can do to increase employees' satisfaction.

Social identity, that part of an individual's self-concept derived from membership in a relevant group, is situationally defined. This concept underscores why it is easy to believe that there is a work version of ourselves and a home version. Context is the main influencer, as it defines how we are seen by the majority in each setting.

While we all belong to multiple groups, including family, community and our workplace, the influence of this construct is dramatically different depending on where you sit within the power pyramid.

For Black women, there is a greater divergence between their 'work self' and the social identity derived from non-work activities and contexts. There is a distinct rift between how Black women are valued within the workplace and their real value outside the workplace. The pandemic has shown that Black women are starting businesses more than any other demographic, but there is more to this than meets the eye. On further analysis, it has come to light that a lot of Black women have had pre-pandemic side hustles but the pandemic gave them the extra push to take them full time.

The question is why? The answer: the value trade-off. Their corporate identity is neither recognized nor seen as valuable and, usually, side hustles provide the value outlet that is often missing in the workplace. This separate identity provides an opportunity to express personal worth free from a professional culture that rests on patriarchy, racism, sexism and misogyny.

In contrast, White women and most men tend to have more fluid social identities, with values and behaviours likely to transcend situations. For Black women, there is often no real correlation between who you are outside work and who you are within it. Existence within a corporate culture with pre-determined criteria regarding who is 'made to succeed' (standards and assumptions that inherently exclude you) is fundamentally oppressive. A social identity derived from a group that devalues you forces a trade-off between your true, whole self and personal values and the constraints of the corporate culture you inhabit.

This is where it becomes critical for companies and organizations to assess and change their culture. Employees who sit at an intersection of any oppressed group or groups are precluded from bringing their whole selves to work, which is to the detriment of employees and employers alike. To perpetuate a culture that ignores or devalues important elements of some employees' being is harmful, wasteful and inequitable.

The common topic of allyship connects to this in surprising ways. Allyship in its simplest form is one individual or group using their voice to uplift and empower others, effectively 'making space' for them. But if the existing corporate culture and hierarchy make it precarious to be an ally, it creates a paradigm – where people are comfortable with being allies in one-on-one situations and voicing support in private but rarely want to provide the same support in public. They understand the context of social identity. They understand their position in the hierarchy and that to be a public ally requires a willingness to push through a different set of barriers, a process that involves their own discomfort.

Organizations need to create a culture wherein social identity is less about hierarchy and more about community. Too commonly, colleagues climb over each other to achieve success, totally aware that men have the greatest advantage, with women relegated to second place, and Black women often entirely outside that window of advancement possibility altogether. Consider the subconscious priming that affirms the social identity created within a corporate culture that is foundationally inequitable. With few if any Black women in positions of power, there is no example of possibility. Conversely, one or a few Black women in leadership may be held up as proof that all it takes is hard work to get to the top (as if these successful Black women didn't have to work harder, longer and better than, for example, a White man would have to do to reach those same heights).

Corporate culture is not passive, and cannot be considered acceptable or just unless the culture and the social identities it fosters match. A culture that forces anyone to behave inauthentically to fit the stereotype applied to them requires deep analysis and meaningful improvement.

There are effective and impactful changes that can be made to increase engagement at every point in the life cycle of an employee, to optimize their experience. For example, when a Black woman interviews at a company, this is the opportunity to make the first impression, but if the person who is supposed to welcome this Black woman in sees her as an intruder, the chances are that the outcome is going to reflect that. She is not going to feel welcome because no one has put the time into understanding context.

We can follow this track of intrusion through each part of the book: from promotion to how Black women are instrumentalized within the business to be members of DEI committees or the chief diversity officer or the leader of a Black employee resource group, yet her needs themselves can still be ignored.

We will look at this through the promotion process. What is the promotion process and how, once again, does it take into consideration the barriers that a Black woman faces in terms of access opportunity and network to move forward?

What resources are you providing above and beyond salary and paying for qualifications? How are you ensuring she's positioned as a member of staff with expertise and not the face of 'DEI' promotion?

Then we will look at gender equity through the eyes of sponsorship and mentoring, at what more is involved and the requirements for those who choose to be sponsors and mentors.

And, finally, we will look at one of the most detrimental and undetected behaviours, for which I have coined the phrase 'exploitative femininity' – a behaviour that endangers Black women, who end up being pushed out of the business by other women if she doesn't follow their rules, and a behaviour that exploits both the patriarchy and racism.

Taking the time to learn about all these behaviours, and understanding how they can be overlooked, is key in repositioning Black women as belonging instead of being intruders. Corporations must also examine the unintended consequences that can further compound the issue when they should be alleviating the burden.

Without being able to recognize how Black women are being positioned in the system, it becomes almost impossible to find solutions to be able to meaningfully include her. Undoing the intruder stances requires a willingness to take action, a willingness to embrace the discomfort and, ultimately, a drive and passion to want to create an inclusive culture by means of specific measures.

So let's take a look at some drivers to career success, why they do not work as linear drivers for Black women, and what gender equity looks like from this standpoint.

CHAPTER THREE

The Hidden Problem with Mentorship and Sponsorship

Mentorship and sponsorship have often been touted as effective solutions for advancing women in the workplace; however, it is important to recognize that these solutions may not be as inclusive and effective for Black women as they are for other groups.

Mentorship can be a valuable tool for developing skills, building networks and gaining access to opportunities, but for Black women, finding a mentor who truly understands their unique experiences and challenges can be difficult. Black women often have to navigate both racial and gender discrimination, and a mentor who is not aware of or sensitive to these issues may not be able to provide the guidance and support that is needed.

Sponsorship is a more formal relationship in which a senior leader advocates for and provides opportunities to a less experienced individual. Sponsorship can be a powerful tool for advancing one's career, but, again, it can be difficult for Black women to find a sponsor who truly understands and is willing to advocate for them.

Moreover, the lack of diversity in leadership roles means that the pool of potential mentors and sponsors for Black women is limited. Black women may find that there are few role models and leaders who look like them, and few people who can truly understand and relate to their experiences.

Returning briefly to the power pyramid, sponsorship between White men and Black women is the least common, according to the *Harvard Business Review* article 'How a Lack of Sponsorship Keeps Black Women out of the C-Suite' in March 2021,[1] so the system is in that sense faulty, because how can Black women make it into those rooms if the powerholders are the ones who sponsor them the least?

There is sometimes a difference between official research and conversations between peers. Anecdotally, I have to admit that having had conversations with many Black women, time and time again what actually does come up is that White men have often been their sponsors even over White women or Black men. One of the things that is rarely if ever talked about with mentorship and sponsorship is the fallout that occurs when a Black woman is sponsored and/or mentored by a senior White male.

Mentorship and sponsorship takes many forms. It can be having dinners, lunches or coffees, and the conversations are not always kept to meeting rooms. Unfortunately, due to the stereotyping around and hyper-sexualization of Black women, jokes and comments can be made that allude to inappropriate relationships and this puts especially junior members in a very precarious position.

The impact of these types of comments are irreversible for Black women in the workplace, especially as they can reach the ears of HR or senior people. It doesn't ever compromise a White man but nearly always compromises the (often young) Black woman in the situation. With stereotyping, prejudice and racism running

---

[1] https://hbr.org/2021/03/how-a-lack-of-sponsorship-keeps-black-women-out-of-the-c-suite

so deep, it is inconceivable for a lot of people that a Black woman is capable of networking above and beyond her 'station', that she is able to be strategic enough to manage her own career. Whether or not it is said in jest, it implies that there is only one currency that she has to trade in and that her looks enable that.

This is one of the issues that companies need to seriously address. It is all well and good encouraging people to have informal mentors and informal sponsors, but the reality is that there is nothing informal about protecting the reputation and career of your mentee. There is a sense of entitlement in a lot of corporates, where everyone expects to be informed about all relationships, but it should not be the expectation.

In lieu of information, mentorship and sponsorship can lead to gossip in a way that is very detrimental to the career of a lot of Black women. It incites jealousy and the fact that it incites jealousy also means that people rely on certain stereotypes, such as the hyper-sexualization of Black women, in order to cause and to propagate trouble. Because once the question has been suggested, it creates a level of possibility and causality in the minds of those who hear the suspicions. People rely on the 'there is no smoke without fire' principle, although in this case, it is nearly always completely wrong.

What makes the situation most tragic is that once it becomes the remit of HR, the damage is done, as there is an obligation to make note of the suggested impropriety even if it is not acted upon. The other part of the danger is that it is easier to believe that the story is true than that someone made it up. There does not always have to be malicious intent, but the jokes and inappropriate conversations still serve the purpose of disparaging and denigrating Black female colleagues, which inhibits their progress within the company.

We may all be colleagues, but at the end of the day, social status and social value are very much determined by those who are in power. And they are also determined a lot of the time by other White men, who sometimes feel slighted by not having what they feel is the same opportunity as this Black woman. Words like 'fairness', 'excessive attention' and 'deserving' are often used in order to make themselves feel better when what they're feeling is racism and sexism. They do not believe that a Black woman deserves the attention of a senior White man who can increase her career chances in the same way he can increase anybody else's career chances. They do not believe it is on merit, but because she is Black and female.

Deeper conversation and analysis around sponsorship and mentorship are required, as the unintended consequences and behaviours can have a counter-productive impact on what sponsorship and mentorship are trying to achieve. These conversations need to take place across all levels of seniority within the business, particularly in the case of C-suite members of staff who tend to be sponsors.

The duty of sponsors and mentors should go further than thinking about the strategic moves that can be made to further her career, but also to protect her from any crosswind, where others compromise her reputation by making innuendos or backhanded comments. It is a sponsor's responsibility to ensure that while they are pushing and breaking down doors within the workplace, there is a broader view that needs to be taken to ensure that she can successfully get through those doors.

It means being aware and taking action against those people who are creating a false narrative and consensus that leads to a movement which inhibits her progress. Being a sponsor or mentor means taking an active role in finding where the seeds of doubt are being sown. The damaging impact on Black women when their reputations are called into question means that taking direct action within a short timeframe is of the essence. There might not be malicious intention behind the gossip, but the outcome is still damaging. As a sponsor or mentor, providing support means taking the situation seriously. These situations escalate into becoming serious with an uncanny speed.

While nepotism works in favour of many non-Black colleagues, this same grace is not applied to a Black woman. The apparent nepotism or favouritism is questioned and her character, credibility and capabilities are doubted. As she begins to succeed with this support, the conversations become granular and comparative, with her whole career being put under the microscope to validate whether she deserves the promotion. 'Is it fair that she is involved in these meetings?', 'Should she be able to work on these types of projects, is it not too soon?' 'Has anyone else made as much progress in the same amount of time?'

In not protecting Black women within this space of mentorship and sponsorship, organizations continue to risk losing an evangelist. It doesn't make any difference how successful a Black woman is within the company. If the reasons for her lack of progression are the result of gossip, rather than her so-called lack of competence, then this could become a contributing factor to her leaving the company. If her success is only contingent upon her ability to make other people feel comfortable with the speed of her progress then it defeats the purpose of her being mentored or sponsored.

The work of wider teams such as Human Resources and Learning and Development is to create support systems that allow her to progress freely, and they themselves have also to come to grips with the fact that the progress of a lot of Black women makes many feel uncomfortable.

Three starting questions for any organization are:

- Do you know how successful mentoring and sponsoring programmes have been within your company for Black women?
- Have you noticed a decrease in the participation of Black women within your company when it comes to mentoring?
- Have you analyzed demographic participation and noticed trends? Is there a representative participation rate in your employee composition?

Getting feedback from Black women in your organization about what their experiences have been in the programmes is key to seeing where you may need to dig deeper in doing more work. Has it led to increased success? Have Black women had to create their own opportunities outside of what was offered? If there is no representative participation, what is the reason for the lack of engagement?

Getting to the root of the issue, if it does not directly benefit Black women in your organization right now, will you help create the infrastructure to support other Black women who will be joining your organization?

It becomes very difficult to question the benefits of mentorship and sponsorship as there are increasingly more examples of why they remain an untapped career booster, but there is yet another factor to both that makes a difference.

Success is still predicated on the creation of opportunity along with the buy-in of others, which can be more a hindrance than a help for Black women. There are five key challenges Black women face within the workplace: stereotyping, visibility and scrutiny, challenge to authority, lack of credibility and exclusion. The role of mentors and sponsors is also to understand how these all have a direct impact on the success of their efforts. A mentor or sponsor can only do so much without this extra knowledge. Recognizing these challenges and then helping their mentees navigate them has a twofold benefit: they will provide more meaningful support with context, but also learn and be able to apply this knowledge of equitable practice within their daily working life.

Let's now look at how some of these challenges can present themselves.

Stereotyping

Stereotyping can present itself in the form of jokes, but also of complaints; the mistaken belief that the only qualifiers to success in this 'woke' era are to be Black and female, that this is the easiest way to get promoted. It also surfaces if she voices concerns, whereupon she can very easily be landed with the reputation of being 'the angry Black woman'. Stereotyping also works in the context of being the antithesis of 'the angry Black woman', when the Black woman is described as being 'not like the others'. This backhanded compliment implies that she is better than the 'standard Black woman', but that is in truth an insult to both her and other Black women.

There will be a stereotype that she will face and, while not all of them will be familiar to her, the ones that she does know about should be discussed, so that mentors and sponsors can learn how it has previously impacted her progression and continues to do so.

Scrutiny and visibility

Black women have flown under the radar in organizations and this has been compounded by the power structure, but the moment they become a mentee or protégée, they automatically come under intense scrutiny. This can come from all quarters, including managers, who may feel slighted and become more critical of the work that is delivered or may even result in them making complaints about her standard of work at appraisal time. Everything she will do from that point on will be adjacent to the question: 'What is it that she has done to deserve being mentored or sponsored above being Black?' Mentors and sponsors need to be prepared not only to initiate these conversations but also actively to find solutions and help her plan a course of action. It is also important that in these discussions the initial reaction is not one that shows doubt in her experience, but that it is embraced.

Challenges to authority

As Black women move up the career ladder, challenges to their authority become more evident. The role of sponsorship and mentorship is then seen as the basis for promotion over hard work and some assistance. The challenge to her authority comes because she is not seen as someone of high potential. This is the exact moment when mentors and sponsors are needed the most, as it may be her peers who are looking to pick holes in her knowledge base and potentially have more power within the organization, which can threaten to undo the hard work she has put in. Research also shows that Black women face the most challenges as managers of teams as they receive not just backlash, but are also subject to internal politics, with complaints going to their managers.

Lack of credibility

In the workplace, Black women may face a lack of credibility in difficult conversations and situations, due to the intersection of racism and sexism they experience. The value of a Black woman's word is often questioned and their ideas and perspectives may be dismissed or ignored. This can make it challenging for them to succeed in their careers and advance in leadership positions.

In these situations, sponsors and mentors can play a crucial role in supporting and advocating for Black women. They can help counteract any questioning of her credibility by providing an endorsement, validating her ideas and perspectives and vouching for her capabilities and expertise.

This can be done by promoting her work and ideas within the organization, as well as actively seeking out opportunities for her to showcase her skills and talents. Sponsors and mentors can also provide guidance and advice to help her navigate difficult situations and conversations, and advocate for her more broadly within the organization.

It is important for mentors and sponsors to recognize the specific challenges that Black women face in the workplace and tailor their support accordingly.

Exclusion

Opportunities as well as the real conversations happen in meetings for the chosen few as well as in informal gatherings. Where has she been left out? Who have been the main people leading this? What has been the impact of this exclusion? Has it been on her career or has it been more that she does not feel like she belongs?

Part of a career progression plan for a Black woman can be mentoring or sponsorship, but it can't be deemed the main source of providing support. The responsibilities of a sponsor or mentor are far more expansive and an organization cannot feel that it has done enough just by creating that opportunity; the other side of the coin is the creation of a conflict point for many people within the company.

This isn't to say that companies cannot offer mentoring or should not promote sponsorship of Black women. It is critical that there is context and conversation on the wider implications of being in this position and the challenges that Black women face. While comments and conversations cannot and should not be policed, a certain level of accountability and responsibility needs to be established to ensure that when a false narrative surfaces it is dealt with swiftly. Taking a clear stance on acceptable behaviours will also create the security for the Black women in your organization that they are not only seen, but heard and respected.

Making this decision means not only that opportunities in her career progression become more stable because there is organizational support and governance to underpin her, but that she is going into a mentorship or sponsorship where both sides are fully informed about the good, the bad and the ugly.

The aim is to provide equitable support, and equity will take more work in order to create those similar opportunities.

Let's now take a closer look and analyze the functions and mechanisms of mentorship and sponsorship, and the potential complications they can create.

Mentorship

I have had great mentors and the most helpful thing when we were in the same organization was that they understood the players involved, and also the strategic goals of the business and the role my department played in those goals. However, at the very beginning of that journey I lacked the language to be able to articulate why my situation was different. I did not have the awareness or, rather, did not want to believe that it could have been because of my race or gender. I put a lot of it down to being young, which meant that some of my frustration was born out of the fact that some of their suggestions were not working and I couldn't see why.

Putting myself in that position now and looking back, even if I knew it was racism and sexism, I would have felt uncomfortable bringing it up, especially if I felt my mentors would not understand. This feeling is still there for a lot of mentees today. They don't want to talk about racism and/or sexism for fear of making their mentors uncomfortable, when the reality is that it affects how they are seen and what they do.

We have women such as Brené Brown and Sheryl Sandberg talking about being courageous and daring to lead and leaning in, all of which are great philosophies, but they do not factor in the five challenges Black women face within the workplace. A Black woman has to plan each interaction with a worst-case scenario mindset because one word taken the wrong way can get her put in the aggressive and not assertive bracket, which quickly changes her career trajectory within the company to being a dead end.

A mentor having the knowledge of the challenges and the impact of those challenges, especially for mentees who may lack the language, can be a complete career changer.

On the other hand, the more prevalent position is that the mentee has both experience and the language and is left with a difficult choice. Does she do the heavy lifting or not?

Either she chooses to educate her mentor, which they may or may not like, or she decides to utilize the information and insights that they have imparted and apply them through the lens of being a Black woman. The problem with the latter option is that in these situations it means that a mentee is never fully a mentee.

There is a burden that has to be carried by the mentee which means that she is never free to share her burden fully, even within the set-up of having a mentor, which is tantamount to more responsibility and an increased emotional load. The role of a mentor is also to try to grasp as much of their mentees' experiences, otherwise the load they carry is that they have to justify their actions and why they need to be both seen and heard.

The approach of mentorship and of mentors and mentees is the defining factor in its success and is where damage can be done through generic mentor programmes. It does not require a mentoring programme just for Black women, but it does require that, if a mentor wants to work with a Black woman, they understand that it is not the same as mentoring others. Specificity in approach and action is critical.

Engaging with the topic will no doubt be uncomfortable for non-Black people, but these challenges prohibit Black women from truly belonging within organizations. Mentoring is more than a nice job to have on a CV or being able to say that it is a way of giving back; it can be life-changing for Black women when done well. By investing in this education for mentors, organizations demonstrate that they are interested and serious about providing suitable support.

Much like client acquisitions, the main exercise that is undertaken is learning what the client's needs are, and it is exactly the same with working with Black women. It is important to see their goals, but also to discuss what the challenges could be that prevent them from achieving them, whether that is the impact of gossip, where they might need extra support, or who they think could be critical in making or breaking their career. A mentor's ability to create a confidential and safe space will take time and the initial phase of mentorship is building the basis of trust before the exchange of information comes. A mentor who shows that they have gone on the journey of growth and learning will significantly speed up the process.

What could go wrong?

We have all been in situations – whether by the coffee machine, at the pub after work or at the lunch table – where we've discussed something that other colleagues have said or done. With all such conversations coming with the caveat 'please don't say anything because I'm not meant to have said this', parts of the conversation nonetheless end up in so many different departments and, irrespective of race, the outcomes of these conversations are never great for the person who is the topic of conversation. People base their judgement of other characters on such stories.

I'll give an example of the impact of these situations. A group of colleagues went out on a weekend and two people in that group had too much to drink and kissed. It was an out-of-office activity in private time, yet news of it made its way into the office and the result was unpleasant. The woman involved in the incident was up for promotion and the situation provoked conversation within the office about her morals and the kind of woman she was, because the man involved had a significant other, and soon descended into a character assassination and conversation about her so-called incompetence. A case study was built that showed she was an unreliable colleague and this incident was used to substantiate this claim. This woman left the business indirectly due to this, but this conversation stopped her promotion possibilities; the fact is that what happened outside work was all of a sudden used as a barometer for her capabilities within the company. Now, she had still managed to be promoted in that time, but her rise was significantly slower. What happened to the man? Nothing. The woman involved was not Black, but she was eventually pushed out of the organization.

In the case of Black women who are highly visible and also subject to scrutiny, these conversations can be detrimental, so while a company may think it is doing a really wonderful thing in setting up a mentoring programme, it can still be undermined by the informal channels of communication and networks within the business that still take this information and then use it in a formal context.

What can never be forgotten is the scale and spectrum of what privilege means. Privilege means not having to think about certain issues – not having to think about your gender, not having to think about your race – a privilege that is not extended to Black women in the first place. But what it means is that she has no scope for error at all, and while careless misinformation should be irrelevant, she does not have that privilege.

The key to equity in mentoring is understanding the starting point, the barriers, the hopes and dreams and desires of Black women within your company, because in doing so you get to know them and you humanize them. Rather than keeping a Black woman as a function, you take the time to make sure that this mentoring programme meets her needs, delivers very specific outcomes and supports her on her journey to thrive in the company.

Sponsorship

The nature of sponsorship is a little bit different. A mentor is someone who guides you to the doors whereas a sponsor is someone who knocks down those doors. In her book *Forget a Mentor, Find a Sponsor*,[2] Sylvia Ann Hewlett says, 'Don't get me wrong, mentors matter. You absolutely need them. They give valuable advice, build self-esteem and provide an indispensable sounding board when you're unsure about next steps, but they are not your ticket to the top.' She's absolutely right. The ticket to the top, as she goes on to say, is a sponsor, someone who 'will smack you harder to shape up … but will protect you as you move to the next level. And will tell you all the sorts of things that were said about you in meetings when you weren't there.'

However, the second half of the quote, describing the role of a sponsor, is a critical part of how I think sponsorship can in many ways go wrong if you don't think about it properly. It's not just about telling somebody what was said about them when they were not in the room. It's about making sure you defend them and also break down the reticence or doubts that these people have about your promotion. The sponsor gets you in the door; the sponsor gets you promoted. The sponsor brings you to dinners well above your paygrade, your sponsor helps you build a

---

[2]*Forget a Mentor, Find a Sponsor: The New Way to Fast-Track Your Career*, Harvard Business Review Press, 2013.

network – all of these are part of creating access and opportunity. But there's one thing that's missing in most of the conversations when they're talking about sponsorship, and it pertains so much to Black women: a sponsor is also responsible for making sure they neutralize any sort of headwinds, remove any inappropriate suggestions and conversations in order to protect her to the fullest. Getting her in the room is an important achievement, but this is where the work begins.

A sponsor's role is also to make sure that the others in those rooms are on their best behaviour because we still have to acknowledge that not everybody is ready for Black women to be in those spaces. The welcome may not be the friendliest from certain people, but it is also the sponsor's responsibility to ensure that she's not facing direct obstruction.

In the settings where she is not present, while it makes sense to know who is not supportive of her being in a particular space, it is critical that when these stories are relayed they form part of a strategy in advising her to navigate the situation. Without creating a plan of action, a sponsor giving this information will lead to insecurity.

Such moments are also when sponsors can use their influence and relationships to get more information on the reasons behind these prejudiced opinions of their colleagues. They may not be able to convince them to change their minds, but there has to be a clear message that they will not be allowed to be obstructive or destructive when it comes to preventing her progress.

With sponsorship and elevation come heightened levels of scrutiny, which can then lead to a pack mentality where Black women, unaware of the unspoken rules, don't realize they are the prey until it is too late. Instead of being happily promoted to her new position, she ends up being a target and constantly has to fight to survive as opposed to working hard to thrive. This is where the equitable part of being a sponsor kicks in.

A sponsor has a lot of weight, power and influence that has to be exerted unilaterally across the board to really drive home to all parties who are interacting with her that they themselves have also to go on a journey, but through process and governance, and that bad behaviour will be penalized.

Sponsors in all cases must play defence and, when it comes to Black women, they also have to play offence. They have to push forward, set the scene; they have to search, to verify and check who else is in the room and what their reputations are. Playing offence means deliberately showing up as real support to ensure that the Black woman isn't being thrown into the lion's den just so that she makes it to the next level. The point of differentiation for successful sponsors is being honest where there is limited capacity to provide suitable support.

It might mean having awkward conversations where a sponsor admits they can only bring their protégée so far; being honest about the lie of the land, which will include naming those who have exhibited racist or sexist behaviours, will ensure that the protégée is prepared. The default in human nature is that when we want to protect someone we make decisions on their behalf and decide where their limitations are. This is no different for a sponsor, but it should not be their decision whether or not she decides to progress. What is absolutely the sponsor's decision is to make sure she is well informed to make that decision, and that she knows who she is dealing with.

The sponsor, if they do not belong to either a minoritized or marginalized group, will have the advantage of hearing more unfiltered opinions from others, especially when she is not in the room, and this is important in giving her the necessary information as she progresses. The conversations in a room filled with White men who are talking honestly will be very different if a Black woman is present as well.

In those meetings, what I'm going to call 'dual listening' is required. The duality is listening to the words that are being said in the context of the topic at hand but also listening to the expressions and the opinions that are being displayed when it comes to racism and sexism so as to be able to identify the people who may be a problem. It's also having the language to navigate these conversations. In this particular situation, a sponsor is also an ally, which will present its own discomfort, but is still very much necessary.

Herein is the critical part of sponsoring Black women. Yes, she's talented, there is no question. Yes, she has absolutely earned her place in the room. There is no question as far as the sponsor is concerned. And this is where offence comes in. And this is where being an ally comes in, too, amplifying the voices of those who are not in the room and don't have the same amount of social capital as they do. This nuance of sponsorship and mentorship and getting it right contributes to the success of efforts. One benefit is that it directly creates evangelists of these women who take part in an efficient mentorship programme or have sponsors and, secondly, it creates mentors and sponsors out of these women, who will then be emboldened to support the next generation.

The next cohort of Black women within companies should be empowered to provide instruction and to share some of the lessons that they've learned from their mentors and sponsors who didn't necessarily face the same issues, and also bring that knowledge to the next generation. This has the compounding, virtuous effect of uplifting, empowering and also adding extra knowledge from rooms that they wouldn't normally have been invited into or would have inhabited.

Inevitably, the following question is going to be asked: if it's so difficult for White men and White women to mentor and sponsor Black women or if their requirements are so high, why don't Black people sponsor or mentor other Black people?

Black people do mentor each other as, ultimately, mentoring is providing a guide. What mentoring does not do is operate on the basis of somebody's ability to influence and have power in the business. Looking at the corporate world at large, this is irrespective of whether it's the UK or the US. Senior Black leaders make up less than 3 per cent of the population and the demographic, which by default means that there is a scarcity mindset rather than an abundance mindset. Questions arise such as 'If I help this person get along what position are they going into?' And the answer they feel they would receive is that this person would be seen as a threat, who would take their position. With a small pool of Black leaders, a business implicitly signals that there is no space for many more, so the two things go hand-in-hand, promoting more Black talent independently of sponsoring to engender more sponsoring between Black colleagues.

Research carried out by the *Harvard Business Review*[3] also found that some of the Black leaders do not necessarily feel that they have the requisite power and social capital to be able to

---

[3]https://hbr.org/2022/02/20-of-white-employees-have-sponsors-only-5-of-black-employees-do

sponsor other talent, because in many ways their position is one of representation as opposed to influence within the business.

We will explore the impact of this on Black women further down the line, but for now the equation I don't want you to forget is:

REPRESENTATION + POWER = CHANGE

To redress this issue of being able to create a situation where Black employees are also empowered to mentor and sponsor Black talent also means looking at the organization and how it's constructed. It means looking at the fact that if Black people are only in senior positions so as to be the face of change, but remain unable to be instruments of change, then this will also have to be analyzed more closely.

In the meantime, it becomes even more important for White sponsors that they not only advocate for their protégées to be recognized and acknowledged, so that they can gain access to more closed rooms, but that they also challenge the existing structure to ensure that when they're bringing these women into these new positions this doesn't fall into the category of 'she is representative and a future role model', and used as a poster child for progress.

She may very well be a future role model, but it should not be forgotten that she has this opportunity because she is qualified and that if it were not for systemic barriers she would not need a sponsor. She should also be empowered by her sponsor's action to operate within an abundance mindset. The failure of sponsorship will be if there is a Black woman at the top who is neither capable of nor willing to help other Black women who come after her because she doesn't feel as if there's any more room for her to progress and grow in the organization. This will break the virtuous effect and undo the good work that any organization does, because their progress starts and ends with one woman, which is neither sustainable nor regenerative in approach.

To go back to the formula, until organizations make space for Black people to have power positions and to be sponsors, it still feeds into White saviourism – that only White sponsors can create a dynamic shift for Black people, when the truth is that the organization is not ready to give Black people power.

The role of sponsorship should be to endorse those who have been overlooked and historically oppressed, not just to give more opportunity to those who happen to be the 'right' gender or race.

Both mentorship and sponsorship provide the opportunity to individually support the Black women in your organization, centre their needs and learn about their challenges, which will not only positively impact their experience within your organization, but will also create more allies out of the mentors and sponsors.

CHAPTER FOUR

The DEI/ERG Positioning

No matter where I turn, there are so many Black women who are happy and proud to be part of a diversity, equity and inclusion committee; the head of the committee leading the charge for an employee resource group; or being in the official role of chief diversity and equity officer, because all these roles have been created with the focus in mind of creating inclusive cultures and organizations.

Yet, there is an increasing bind to these positions, an uncomfortable truth, which is that as long as Black women are willing to play ball and follow the rules, and stay within particular parameters that don't rock the boat too much and that don't require too much change and also don't focus too much on Black women, their ascent to the top and journey to acceptance will be smoother. Their chances of success are tied to their ability to maintain this very particular mandate.

However, problems are increasingly developing, because when the gloss wears off as organizations move into action mode, they are still stuck in the planning phase. This causes frustration as these women want to do more than just be a face, especially as they took the position in order to drive equitable change within the company that would directly benefit other Black women and not just themselves.

Yet when they do that, the pushback becomes real.

In the last two years, these diversity, equity and inclusion positions have felt like the recognition of the work that these women have been putting in on top of their day jobs, and organizations have claimed that these roles would be setting them up for success.

It has felt like a dream position and opportunity. The creation of all these diversity, equity and inclusion committees created the feeling of change, progress and momentum, which of course led to people feeling bolstered and empowered by all of it, but now disappointment and reality are beginning to set in.

Referring to the McKinsey Women in the Workplace report, Black women have been identified as the demographic with the most ambition,[1] so when you combine the opportunity to address injustice within the workplace and Black women's ambition, what you get is a powerful catalyst and a powerful combination. This has the potential to create real impact within organizations, but what has often happened instead is that the ambition of Black women has been exploited and their organizations remain unwilling to prioritize their needs.

How can support turn into exploitation?

It does not start out as exploitation on the organization's side. There is a genuine desire and drive to create change. This usually means that they ask Black women to increase their visibility, which is often in the form of being the face of the DEI movement within their organization, speaking externally on

---

[1]https://leanin.org/research/state-of-black-women-in-corporate-america/introduction

panels to represent their companies on a wide range of topics, varying from where their original expertise started to the plans of the company. The problems arise when Black women begin to hold their organizations accountable and want them to take action on behalf of Black people or Black women. The moment an organization refuses or typically delays taking action is the moment that support becomes exploitation. All the benefits accrue to the organization, as they are given reputational points for the display of diversity, while not doing anything internally.

Black women at the forefront – not just for DEI, to show that they are experts in their field above and beyond being Black women – is a reputational win for organizations. Having a Black female advocate especially at senior level creates the impression of the company being a safe space for Black women.

Companies continually collect a dividend based on the appearance of them being diverse because at a time when there is heightened awareness around racism, sexism and misogyny, the easiest way for these companies to show that they're taking any kind of action is to have a Black woman's face front and centre.

The situation does not seem extractive because these women believe the reciprocal support to create change is there – and why wouldn't they? In the earnestness of wanting to make change and in the belief that change is going to come, these companies have exploited the premise of what these Black women believe in. Many organizations promised the world and committed both internally and externally that, within the next two years, they were going to do many things; ultimately, though, they reneged on that promise, which has had a devastating effect on many Black women reputationally who have been the face of the initiatives.

The lack of support, the pushback and the internal mechanics are not seen externally, which means Black women rather than the organizations can be held accountable, thus compounding the questioning of their capabilities.

Once again, context is everything; as part of the knee-jerk reaction to George Floyd's murder, many organizations started out with quite specific initiatives focused on Black people within the workplace but soon the plans became more diluted into being a generic DEI initiative.

But before we can move on to the impact generic DEI initiatives have on the values of Black women who are charged with being DEI or ERG leaders, we have to unpick why these initiatives became less specific.

There is the discomfort in talking about race, but there is another often-ignored issue: the fear of Black people coming together within the corporate space.

For the longest time, I could never understand the fascination around a group of Black professionals coming together, why it was commented on and observed. The interrogation that would follow: 'How do you know them?', 'Did you know them before here?', 'I didn't think you worked with them because you never mentioned it.' The list of questions is endless. The intrigue and suspicion were palpable.

Why were they scared, and what were they trying to find out?

Returning to the 'intruder' context, seeing camaraderie is uncomfortable. It creates community and this is a source of fear for many. They fear that these relationships are not based on friendship, professional relationships and joy, but on something more sinister.

The desire to maintain the power structure underpins the discomfort of seeing Black women come together, who could mobilize a movement within the organization.

Professional gaslighting has made Black women believe, on an individual level, that they are the reason they are not making the progress that they should be. The lie of meritocracy can be sold on an individual basis, but it cannot be true when an entire demographic shares the same experience. When more Black women come together, to exchange and learn from each other, the institutional barriers cannot be ignored.

Acknowledging this internal fear on both an individual and institutional level can be horrifying, when the roots of this feeling are based on racism and it is societal conditioning that has rationalized and justified it.

It's important for companies to understand that simply having a diverse workforce or implementing a few diversity and inclusion initiatives is not enough to truly create a culture of equity and inclusion. You must be willing to address the specific issues and barriers that Black women face in the workplace, and take a targeted and deliberate approach to addressing them. This means acknowledging and addressing the ways in which systemic racism and discrimination have impacted Black women, and not just relying on general diversity and inclusion efforts that may not address these specific issues.

Being courageous also means being willing to take a hard look at your organization as well yourself individually, to acknowledge inherent biases and shortcomings and to take concrete and specific actions to address the barriers that Black women face in the workplace. Introspection will assist chief diversity officers, heads of diversity, equity and inclusion committees and employee resource groups to be as effective as required.

This fear of Black women coming together also drives the company's avoidance of allowing them to be the driving force behind Black female-focused initiatives internally. The Black female employee's position as an external representative will give her more flexibility, as it directly impacts the firm's reputation.

When she is allowed to be the external face, but cannot help other Black women internally, this undermines her integrity and her motivation. The organization demands more of her because it understands the power of having a Black woman in high – profile positions and the reputational benefits it gives. Yet this has breached her trust in the company and its integrity.

How can she still feel protected and confident about her own growth potential when the measure of her success is based on her ability to deliver on DEI topics, but her ability to focus on certain groups, including Black women, is limited within the organization?

The dream position soon becomes the nightmare position. She can talk about everything but race. It makes her want to engage less in the organization, as she has gone from believing it was part of the overall DEI plan to seeing the deliberate avoidance of supporting Black women. There is pushback, with excuses being made related to budgets or timing.

She now only serves the position of being a representative without power, so she cannot fulfil the role that she wanted to. Although there is no explicit demotion, getting pushback and not being able to determine her budget allocation or programme timing contributes to her feeling devalued.

She will chastise herself for being naive: naive to believe that the company was really going to deliver on their promise this time. That she was blind to their exploitation of her ambition, which made her believe she had influence, was valued and that her contribution would drive change. Instead of being a gamechanger, she simply does not know how to proceed. Does she try to turn things around in her organization or does she try to find another job, one where she will have to take responsibility for the lack of progress that was not her fault?

The damage does not stop at the professional part; it also has a psychological impact. The organization had crafted an optic and awarded her a senior title, but not a senior role.

This has all the trademarks of professional gaslighting. It can make her doubt her ability to succeed in the role, when on paper nothing has changed, but in reality this is because her powers have been all but rescinded, when it matters the most.

This is where it becomes difficult for her to stay within the company because, while the organization is being recognized for being an industry leader in diversity, equity and inclusion, being recognized as a great place for women to work, what she knows in reality is that it is not true. But at the same time, she's still being asked to promote and sign off on the company's ability to deliver.

Knowing the impact of the power structure on the behaviour of Black women and the need to feel like a cultural fit, the worst accusation that can be levelled against a Black woman is of being unprofessional. She knows how hard it is to build a good reputation and how easy it is to lose it and this is leveraged against her as another layer to the exploitation.

If she actively refuses to be a part of the charade, she is still aware of the price that she will have to pay and that she will give licence to the conversations that later 'justify' the exclusion of Black women in power rooms – with the accusation 'well, we gave these Black people the opportunity to make changes, but as soon as things became difficult, they decided to step back'.

How can she extricate herself from the situation and do the least damage to other Black women in the company and herself? Can she step back, leaving her open to accusations of leaving the movement, or does stay true to her values? Will she have to give up her ambition? Will she be tarnished with the brush of not being a team player? How will she get a similar role if she cannot prove her success in her existing role?

This is the reality of the burden and the situation Black women are left in, when organizations do not actively follow through on their promises and prevent them from driving change. The impact of this also gravely damages the chances of other Black women who may want to enter the organization.

Exploitation of the Black woman's ambition is a blind spot, as many do not see the deeper damage they are doing. The appreciation of her willingness is gradually taken for granted without understanding the premise of her willingness. She is dedicated to the cause. They know that they are focused on window dressing by having Black people feature in their marketing materials or that there is a strategy behind the selection of Black women to talk about their company to highlight any part of their business. They do not see and acknowledge the exploitation of Black women in externally high-profile positions.

It is critical that your organization recognizes that there is a responsibility to support Black women who are in DEI roles. Exposure does not guarantee career success and should not be relied on and the main benefit to being in this position. The role should benefit not only your organization, but also needs to contribute to her success.

How can your organization support Black women who are in DEI roles? Answer some of these questions:

- Have your deliverables for the chief diversity officer changed from the point she accepted the job?
- Who is the source of the pushback that prevents her from doing her job?
- Have you kept as much of a focus on racial equity since 2020 up until now?
- Have you delivered on the commitments you made to Black employees, customers and within the supply chain since 2020?

Answering these questions honestly will help you to diagnose and assess where you might be unintentionally doing more damage than good.

Not all the women who are externally high profile are necessarily senior within the business. They may win awards for their work with DEI committees and employee resource groups.

Having spent time working with a lot of employee resource groups/DEI committees, one thing is clear to me. There is employee resource group/DEI committee fatigue, which has set in due to the considerable investment of time and energy with next to no results.

A lot of Black women are being penalized financially and by reduced career opportunities in the parts they play within these committees and groups. The assumption is that most people have the support of their managers, but in the Experience Chasm Survey 2021 we also discovered that one of the most significant barriers was managers.[2] More than 55 per cent of respondents had the most pushback from their managers. Many of the respondents' managers felt that activism should take place in their own time rather than the company's, and that it played no meaningful role in the direction the company was taking.

Without managerial support, women who are DEI committee and ERG members are forced into proving that their equity work is valuable and that it is not impacting their day job, while often not receiving explicit support from leaders and senior management. An organization's decision to be transparent regarding not only the importance of equity work, but also its relevance to overall business strategy, defines the tone within the organization and its people leaders. Without DEI having strategic relevance and being a priority in their organizations, these women are left exposed.

Their manager may fail to see why this is important, especially if the most senior members of the organization don't; all they see is the DEI/ERG work encroaching on the employee's work, which can lead to direct and indirect complaints that they are not performing satisfactorily (which can also be expressed in the lack of a pay rise, bonus or promotion).

To ensure that she is protected, there needs to be clear communication from senior leadership that is also reaffirmed by all levels of management. The importance of her work will be diminished if all the communication takes place behind closed doors – it needs to be openly acknowledged.

---

[2]https://www.benefactumconsulting.com/closing-the-chasm

When you get to this point, the question for any organization is:

- Am I making sure that when Black women are participating in DEI committees or ERGs they are protected and have the support that they need?

This means that setting up a committee or an employee resource group should not be a knee-jerk reaction that exploits the fact that there are many Black women willing to be part of it and to take the internal movement further.

Further questions are:

- How do we ensure that her objectives are not compromised?

This means creating clear guidelines from the committee or ERG perspective that outline the time requirements and talk about the impact and target adjustments that will ensure that she is not penalized. This cannot just be signed off by her immediate manager, but has also to involve the person responsible for setting the budget and the most senior person in the department, to ensure that all decision-making parties are aware of her involvement. They must also provide as much transparency as possible, such as setting clear expectations with, for example, the difference in the time commitments between being the chair of the committee versus being a volunteer. There might be a negotiation period, but the aim is that Human Resources and/ or leadership and development take the lead in forming these processes, not the woman.

- Have you been clear that this work is critical to the business, and, most importantly, if so, why?

If this work really is critical to the business, then there can be no doubt about the importance of her being part of a DEI committee or ERG. The opportunity to create change has to be exactly that: an opportunity. There is a fine line between the belief that someone is a changemaker rather than an activist, and while it should not make a difference, it does. As soon as it is perceived that she is an activist, or that she is doing more than she should, or that she is too vocal, she ends up in the unfortunate position where the space for her to be herself and to progress becomes infinitely smaller. The opportunity essentially becomes a straitjacket that she can no longer move in, and also no longer get out of.

DEI committees and employee resource groups are comprised of passionate people who want to make change within the organization, but if they are not empowered with the resources to achieve this, companies are creating a career deathtrap, especially for Black women.

LinkedIn is a prime example of where you can see Black women as champions of their organizations, who give them praise, but it begs the question: are they advocating in hopes of seeing change – or because they have already begun to see it?

The exposure and profile carrot can be very alluring, when as a Black woman you have been mostly ignored, so for HR managers, chief diversity officers and chief strategy officers it is important to ask yourself: have you built a trade-ahead strategy, asking Black women to do the legwork to try and build momentum first, to then discuss specifics later?

If so, then the strategy will fail. If the start is conditional and opportunistic, the success in the long term will negligible. Going back to using Black women as a function, rather than focusing on their needs, means that instead of retaining them, organizations will lose the most motivated and most inclined to engage members. Once the reality is clear, the countdown has started.

The problem is rarely that there is not enough Black female talent, but, rather, the ones who are there lack the support and infrastructure to be able to thrive. If a company is really serious about making their environment and their culture one that enriches Black women, then the set-up of committees and employee resource groups has to be just as strategic.

I have defined three pillars that underscore successful employee resource group or DEI committees, and they are:

1) celebration
2) complaint
3) strategy

The *celebration* part is the easiest to achieve, as even if there are educational elements the main goal is to have fun and celebrate minoritized and marginalized groups. There is no discomfort in this part of the itinerary, and as such it can lead to an overemphasis on the fun. This can result in the misconception that these initiatives lack substance, when that is far from the truth.

The ability to register and discuss *complaints* is equally important, as this creates space to learn what can be done better, and where the weaknesses are within teams and the organization. What makes both of these pillars more cohesive is strategy.

The *strategy* pillar is the one that ensures that meetings are not useless, that there is governance in place to encourage participation, organize great events, but also to ensure that the goals of the groups are aligned with the overall business goals. An ERG or DEI committee without strategic alignment is as useful as a blunt knife. Being aligned also means that the groups will be taken more seriously by the more sceptical members of staff, who think it is all a bit of a jolly and an excuse to get out of doing work.

Governance around participation mitigates the risk of Black women being penalized in their day jobs. Clear strategy gives comfort that there is a tangible benefit to this, not just because everyone is jumping on the bandwagon. Not only that, but clearly aligned strategy further promotes the belief that the Black women in these committees and groups have broader expertise, rather than just being seen through the lens of lived experience.

Using good governance to create equitable and sustainable processes should help to remove the unnecessary burden of having to manage upwards and deal with systemic barriers while being an agent of change.

Never has there been a time like the present when being a Black woman is to be hot property. It is almost the best it can be in terms of visibility, yet, despite this, the levels of exhaustion, disappointment and frustration are at an all-time high because change is not trickling through businesses in the way it should be. The powers that be determined they would do things differently after posting black squares on social media and signing commitments and pledges and charters. They promised their culture was going to change and Black women jumped in with both feet, only then to be tied up.

What still keeps Black women going?

One of the key and almost overwhelming data points from the Experience Chasm Survey 2021 was that of the 104 women surveyed over 80 per cent of them still confirmed that they believed that their organization still had an opportunity and a chance to create cultures that allowed Black women to thrive. And in most cases, that was down to their own involvement in wanting to make sure the company did right by Black people and Black women but also through fundamental trust, and belief in good old human nature.

We have established that there is a willingness to work, that there is ambition to improve the workplace, so the missing factor is that Black women have not been set up for success. These Black women in the context of their roles in ERGs and DEI committees are delivering to the extent permitted and the prohibition is contingent on how serious the business is in providing support for them in these roles.

Even within this context, privilege has different outcomes. White women are afforded the opportunity of using their time working with ERGs and DEI committees to build careers in a field where they lack expertise, but they are given that chance based on potential and passion. The messenger in the corporate can be more important than the message, and with Black women having the double outsider status, they are not included in critical meetings to make the same jump.

The voice of Black women and their input gets drowned in non-promotable tasks that would not allow her the same chance to jump into a fully-fledged career in DEI, even if she wanted to. Her work has to be seen as valued and that this contributes to her development and growth. Praise has its place, but there is still a big difference between *making* somebody feel as though what they're doing is important and *showing* them that what they're doing is important. Money is a significant way to show appreciation, but in daily business there are many more ways.

Support is ensuring that senior management not only buys into any strategic plans by signing off budgets, but that they take an active role in being a buffer against difficult conversations with their direct managers. In situations where a manager challenges their contribution, that is, the perceived diminished contribution, it is vital that senior management provide additional support in overseeing the pay rise, bonus and promotion process to ensure that they are not being unduly penalized.

It is not the responsibility of Black women to be the external face and the internal engine without meaningful support. This also means providing her with the opportunity to engage an external coach or mentor, paid for by the organization, to help her discuss the emotional load of the work she is doing.

From CDO to DEI/ERG group members, the emotional load that Black women carry in these roles is immense, as they are working to solve issues that also affect them professionally. Setting them up for success reiterates the concept of the human over function – they need to be provided with the emotional support to be able to do their job.

The impact of lacking support affects the mental health and wellness of these women, which means that they end up either suffering from some sort of burnout or are forced to hide behind working from home in order to avoid being faced with their daily, weekly or monthly disappointments.

In a misguided attempt to show progress, it is not uncommon for women in these positions to be sold as a saviour, and when they are not able to deliver effectively according to their standards, they carry the extra sense of responsibility of having let down other Black women within their organization. The precarious position they are put in means that their ability to deliver on promises or goals, made in good faith based on information that they had been given by senior people, has been impeded.

When she is put in the position in which she has overpromised and underdelivered, the damage is far-reaching. This behaviour is seen as a betrayal, which irrevocably breaks trust within the Black community internally, as it begins to raise questions, such as if those who look like them do not deliver and do not seem to see the importance of DEI, how will those who don't?

Putting Black women in high-visibility and high-responsibility positions may seem like a great strategic move for your organization, but, as discussed here, there is not only a wider context, but scope to do damage if it is not considered and executed meaningfully.

CHAPTER FIVE

The Black Superwoman Benchmark

We spoke previously about the mechanism of the Black woman benchmark as a method of control, but there are ways in which companies unintentionally get it wrong. For Black women it is a known topic, for organizations less so. This is the Black superwoman within a company, where she is held up as the prime example of what is achievable so long as other Black women are prepared to work as hard.

Many organizations fail to recognize that this is still part of the meritocracy fallacy. The story usually lacks the details and this might mean that she did not have the expected struggle narrative, but came from a wealthy family; this does not mean she did not face racism or sexism, simply that the story is nuanced. It may not have been hard work alone that got to her to this place.

Overcoming adversity is the comfortable story that people like to hear because it plays into the narrative that Black women also come from a particular social background. Having to climb out of the gutter on to corporate glory is the best triumph over adversity story and helps to support the belief that other Black women can do that, too.

There is another reason why details are avoided. Unpacking her success requires addressing a lot of issues that the company doesn't necessarily want to face. Focusing on the effects of luck and timing as well as her ability to deliver on a job creates a false sense of possibility.

The conversations about the challenges she has faced are usually curated for internal blogs and external interviews, which in and of itself is not problematic, but when there is a clear steer away from discussing sexism and racism it prioritizes the brand over her experience.

The priority of brand protection obscures probing questions, such as: What did it take for this woman to make it to the top of the business? What was it that she sacrificed and what were the obstructions or who were obstructive in her reaching that point?

There is a tendency to romanticize her story and to avoid discussing the challenges she may have faced due to a bad culture or poor governance. Omitting these details helps her organization to circumvent accountability and a need to change. The effect of this is that Black women in the organization are burdened with the belief that they are more than likely the problem, rather than the corporate culture being the issue. Without organizational accountability, the narrative that all it takes to be successful is hard work is supported.

In many ways, the superwoman benchmark is the easiest mechanism for gaslighting other Black women. The successful Black woman is not the problem. This cannot be emphasized too strongly. The problem is that companies instrumentalize her position. They use her as an example of representational possibilities but at the time silence Black women because there is discouragement from talking about sexism and racism.

To meaningfully engage with her means that organizations have to start to encourage multi-layered conversations that include successes and challenges.

Nothing has been more powerful than Roz Brewer, CEO of the Walgreens Boots Alliance, discussing her experiences of discrimination and why she advocated for diversity in 2021. She spoke for so many Black women who had experienced discrimination, too. She is the antidote to this superwoman benchmark. She is one of only two Black female CEOs of a Fortune 500 company and has shown that her success did not protect her from discrimination.

Discrimination, however, is not the only critical factor standing in the way of Black women's success. It can also come from other women. This is where exploitative femininity starts and can be a career ender for many if it is not recognized and sufficient action taken.

What is exploitative femininity?

I coined the phrase 'exploitative femininity' in the summer of 2021 as I realized that there was a very specific behaviour that undermines not just gender equality efforts, but impacts the career chances of Black women and is for the most part ignored by men in the workplace.

This toxic behaviour flies under the radar and for this reason it is important to get to grips with the behaviour and how dangerous it really is.

Later in the book we will look at strategies for combatting this on both an individual and an organizational level.

But first let's jump straight into it.

Before we can delve into the depths of this topic, we have to be myth busters, especially when it comes to women and womanhood and our ideas about sisterhood.

Myth #1 is the belief that all women belong to an unspoken, universal sisterhood whose members rally around and support each other in all situations. This myth brings visions of cheering teammates fighting side by side, striving as a unit to achieve gender equality, and that the cause means the same thing to all of us.

Myth #2 is that women who act or appear traditionally feminine (whatever that may mean in a given time and place) or are perceived as very feminine (with the same caveat) need to be protected, saved and helped because they are weak and deserve special treatment.

This second myth is insidiously intertwined with the first in professional and work scenarios as well as in everyday life. Both have as much to do with how men perceive women as with how women see themselves, as individuals and as part of a defined class.

Embracing these myths is common, and dangerous. The element of exploitation arises when individuals masquerade as warriors for equity, dedicated to uplifting others, when in fact they are positioning themselves for personal gain by channelling the very myths surrounding femininity they pretend to despise. Often these women consciously project (especially to men) an aura of traditional femininity — all sweetness and light, dependable but non-threatening. She is the 'good girl' that those in power can point to as evidence of their efforts towards workplace equity without actually taking concrete steps towards that goal. It's all a show, and involves predictable patterns of behaviour in which a perpetrator casts herself as the victim, triggering the expected response of powerful men in her defence.

Consider the following stories: unfortunately you will probably find them familiar.

A new woman enters the workforce and starts out on good terms with her colleagues. She is capable, dedicated and determined to work hard and advance her professional standing. What she may not know is that among her workgroup is a woman skilled in the charade of exploitative femininity. At some point, the new employee questions a process, suggests an improvement, or shines in an unexpected way. The 'good girl' feels threatened, and reacts in one of two predictable ways, similar in purpose but with slightly different tactics, both designed to maintain her superior standing and ensure her professional ascent.

The first tried-and-tested scenario involves specific complaints made directly to management and/or Human Resources. The new colleague is accused of being too aggressive or direct, or of intentionally wresting the focus from the 'good girl', leaving her feeling isolated or undermined by the interloper. She may present these complaints sweetly, allowing that the new colleague may just not understand 'the way things are done' in this environment. Whatever the dramatic twist, these complaints often succeed in eliciting the protective impulses of those in power. They will not allow this brash new employee to bully their favourite; her carefully constructed illusion of victimhood serves her well.

The second method involves crowd-sourcing the abuse of the new colleague with an internal campaign against her. Cliques form, selective (dis)information is shared with specific people, the atmosphere in the office gets progressively chillier. The new colleague is isolated by this behaviour. Her progress is stymied and her recourse is limited. By the time she realizes the level of co-ordination against her and approaches management, Human Resources or a (hopefully) trusted colleague or mentor, it's too late. She has already been painted as the aggressor or, worse, the disruptor. It is often now only a matter of time before she leaves the company.

The first phase is preparation.

This is the most dangerous part of the whole behaviour as it is fundamental to an exploiter's ability to fully execute the plan in the event that she needs to. This is her insurance. There is no guarantee that this behaviour will change into exploitative femininity as long there is no turning point.

Friendship – the potential exploiter will without doubt be one of the first people to invite you to coffee and offer to show you the ropes. But what seems to be a genuine offer of help is really a red flag. She will brief you on who you should avoid. We instinctively begin to trust people who take us into their confidence and she understands this precept perfectly. This is an assault on your ego because it is human nature to feel flattered that you are being included, and pleased or relieved that you are getting the real scoop. This is part of the trap; you will probably respond by sharing with her your first impressions of other people, thereby giving her even more insight into your thoughts and what she perceives as weaknesses she can later exploit.

Ownership – once your friendship has been solidified, her next step is to flaunt it publicly. She will take you under her wing and begin to act as your introducer, subtly influencing the creation of your new professional network.

Claiming you as her friend entices you to become reliant on her as you will start to build a network that is heavily intertwined with hers or heavily connected to yours. This forms the basis of the point of isolation.

Professional mentor – she will become your self-appointed mentor, which will help her position herself as a key person in your professional advancement. Insidiously, this will also serve to create the perception that you need help, even when that is not the case, damaging your reputation, your potential and perhaps even your self-confidence.

Your reaction here will also inform her of your tendency towards what she thinks of as loyalty. She is setting the stage for future behaviours and counting on you not to mention questionable ones to anyone else.

Turning point – this can be the culmination of an exploiter's long-term plan and the point at which her groundwork begins to pay off. You may have an actual disagreement, but usually the turning point is more benign. She may hear from too many people (for her comfort) that you are doing a good job or that you are liked and respected. This is where she begins to activate the second part of her plan.

Sowing the seeds of doubt – the exploiter will start to have discussions with your mutual network, in which she doesn't say anything explicitly negative, but will intentionally raise questions or make insinuations that encourage colleagues to jump to the conclusion she wants. This is where the attack on your credibility and ability starts.

Isolation – now that the ground is fertile for you to become the object of dislike or distrust, the exploiter will begin to speak more openly about your behaviour from the beginning. In conversation, she will paint the picture that, despite her best efforts and helpful mentoring, you really don't belong in your position and are not an asset to the team. You will begin to notice that your colleagues are acting strangely towards you and you feel tension … but you don't know why.

Confrontation – since you have been groomed to trust the exploiter, you will confide in her your feelings of isolation, thinking she can help you understand the change in attitude among your colleagues. She will repeat this conversation to your boss and other colleagues, framing it in a way that intimates that she felt attacked and suggesting that maybe 'someone' should talk to you.

This part of the process solidifies you as an outsider: unreasonable, aggressive and simply not the right fit for the team. It also ensures that you have no one on your side who is willing to listen to you objectively and act as your ally.

The end game

The complaint – either your boss or someone from Human Resources will call you in for an informal chat centred around reports they have heard that, despite their genuine best efforts to help you integrate with the team and succeed in your role, your colleagues feel bullied, victimized or scared of you. They will express a willingness to hear your side of the story, but it becomes clear that others have joined the chorus of complaints or will back up the original complaint made by an unnamed individual. You are, of course, left blindsided and wondering where this has come from, so let's explore this process further and identify actionable strategies for how you can defend yourself. However, before we do that, let's look at some of the ways this behaviour is inadvertently supported by existing societal structures.

How this behaviour is supported by:

The patriarchy and racism

Many intrinsic elements of patriarchal society allow for exploitative femininity to go undetected. The added effects of systemic racism and gender bias combine to make exploitative femininity particularly damaging to Black women. Although it's tempting to deal with racism separately as it connects to this behaviour, the nature and ubiquity of patriarchy make it impossible to entirely disentangle the two. When we think of intersectionality (*see* p.104), namely being a Black woman, we must acknowledge that Black women experience the effects of racism and patriarchy concurrently, and that the damage of each therefore compounded.

Patriarchal society dictates that men are and should be both dominant and privileged, and thus rightfully belong at the top of the hierarchy of power. The traditional role of women, in society, history and literature, was both domestic and subservient. There have been, of course, notable exceptions, such as Queen Victoria, whose royalty was hers by birth as opposed to being the result of marriage … but, that said, her power was still by birthright rather than an individual achievement.

In earlier centuries, ambitious and successful women were often described as using the 'man's part' of their brain. Stereotypically, society's concept of an ideal woman has been wrapped in the identity of some tangential outcropping of a man. She placated and served, and had no ideas of her own. The 'good girl' we've discussed as an exploiter is a modern version of this. She is willing to incorporate men's egos into the decisions she makes, bowing to authority (or at least appearing to), knowing that patriarchy will define her success as how men see her. This benchmark exists to this day, in personal and romantic relationships, and very much in the professional setting as well.

We have all been conditioned by this patriarchal thinking. The 'good girl' is considered such because she doesn't cause trouble or make demands. She goes with the flow, and agrees with the opinions of the powerful men in her life. When acting in the realm of exploitative femininity, she seems malleable but is actually calculating and manipulative. She plays a particular role not because she isn't bright enough to discern its shallowness, but because it is a means to an end.

Periods of flaunting this worldview have been met with a backlash. Remember in the 1980s, when women with professional white-collar careers were expected to dress like men? In order to succeed, the well-dressed professional climber wore suits in dark colours, cut like the men's, and even with padding in the shoulders to enhance the disguise. It was colloquially thought to be an advantage that would help women succeed in what was still very much a man's world. It was, however, a veneer – really a ploy – that did not change patriarchy. A masculine wardrobe often brought ridicule and heckling because most men were offended that women dared to try to 'be' men. In a word, they were threatened.

Hence, exploitative femininity, wherein the 'good girl' realizes that her best chance of ascending is by staying under the radar. Playing along with what the patriarchy expects and can accept of a woman, she becomes almost a caricature. Add racism to the mix and things get even more ugly and complicated.

The hierarchy of society and corporate and economic power forms a pyramid, as mentioned in the first chapter.

This dynamic creates, reinforces and maintains stereotypes. In the current discussion, among the most damaging stereotypes applied to a Black woman is that she is an aggressor. This plays into the 'good girl's' accusations of bullying, her cry to her network of powerful men for protection. This assumed aggressor status also makes it nearly impossible for a Black woman to use exploitative femininity to her advantage. Not seen as vulnerable, she cannot weaponize her tears the way our (White) 'good girl' can.

Constructs of slavery, segregation and discrimination have embedded this dichotomy. The White woman is vulnerable, her chastity requires protection, she deserves to be accommodated. Exploitative femininity in the professional office is founded upon the same dynamic historically used to justify lynchings, particularly in the American South in the twentieth century. Simultaneously, the Black woman is dehumanized into an aggressor. There is no framework in which she can portray herself as fragile, a vulnerable 'good girl'. No one believes that she could just be nice, malleable, friendly, non-threatening and all the other things that through the lens of the men at the top of the pyramid would make her a 'good woman'.

So how does this play out in the modern professional office? The tropes are always a benchmark. Through the existing patriarchal and racist lens of most at the top of the hierarchy, Black women are assumed to be aggressive, difficult and any number of other negative stereotypes. White women (that is, those willing to engage in exploitative femininity) at least have the option of adopting the 'good-girl' persona. They start out with access to a trick not available to all women. And then Black women and White women are pitched against each other. By default, the Black woman will be portrayed as angry and defiant, but never vulnerable; the White woman is a 'good girl'. It does not matter who is actually right or wrong in the workplace, the outcome cannot be good, or equitable, or fair.

The White woman who chooses to play the role of the 'good girl' harnesses the protective impulses of White men (who are higher up the power pyramid). They like her, and will contribute to her success. This does not come without personal sacrifice. Her obstruction of other women's progress and her manipulative behaviour require her to be someone other than who she really is because she has made a conscious decision to adopt this strategy. Her skill at deception makes detection difficult, and because she is perceived as being nice, accommodating and non-threatening, the rest of the workplace often does not realize the sinister plans below the surface of her reputation.

For Black women, for whom stereotypes block the 'good-girl' role – even if they would choose that path – the more likely option is to try to fit in. New to any office, Black women feel the need to diminish their Blackness, to fade into the background and fit into the corporate culture. They need to adapt to the standards defined by and for White men in order to succeed. This very act of attempting to fit in is detrimental. She is not free to be as strong, brilliant and confident because she has to waste time and emotional energy amending her true self for greater likeability in an unwelcoming environment.

This is why we must focus specifically on dismantling both gender inequality and racial injustice in the workplace. Reliance on the benchmarks and standards created by and for men, for their own good, hurts all women, but Black women most of all. The (White) 'good girl' understands the power of racism and stereotypes, and can harness the power of the very systems that have created secret but very potent barriers to Black women's professional success. She can exploit that knowledge, playing her role to leverage what she has in common with the power structure to get ahead. She understands that for many corporate leaders there's a basis of fear and misunderstanding, but also a very strong pull to avoid trying to get to know people who are in any way different from them. The denial of humanity and commonality widens into a chasm and creates fertile ground for exploitative femininity.

Today, a lot of leaders indicate that they feel attacked for being White, and male, and for living and working in a manner that does not support gender and/or racial equality. In many ways, ambitious women of any colour are challenging their worldview by pushing for more than what the hierarchy long ago decided they deserve or have any right to expect, much less demand. Enter the exploitative 'good girl', who understands the tension within this situation, and is willing to use the systemic inequities and personal insecurities of powerful men for her own advancement. She surrenders her membership in the (mostly) mythical sisterhood for personal gain, making the workplace even more dangerous and less equitable for her Black counterparts. As long as the patriarchy remains intact and in charge, exploitative femininity will exist – unless we collectively recognize the harm it does and develop strategies to eliminate it.

Corporate culture

As patriarchy and racism form the backdrop of the workplace, corporate culture acts as a wheel, turning continually to maintain the status quo. The seemingly immutable order of things – the hierarchy defined by and for White men – frames appropriate professional behaviour in terms of women assimilating themselves into the existing corporate context, not as actors who can and should help it evolve into a better space. When we analyze success, networks and the possibility for promotion, we often use terms like 'cultural fit' and assign credibility to vague assessments of likeability. The 'good girl' knows this and recognizes the value of being perceived as easy to get along with, even if that designation signifies a way of being that accepts and assimilates rather than any actual trait of being genuine or caring about her colleagues and workplace.

The male-centric worldview upon which a corporate culture generally stands allows for organizations and management to judge (and often dismiss) women's behaviour and interactions as emotional and personal. Despite the intricately strategic nature of exploitative femininity, corporate culture helps hide and preserve this toxic behaviour by relegating it to the heap of 'women's issues' that don't require deep analysis or action. The common association of toxic, heavy-handed and aggressive behaviour with masculinity creates the perfect opening for exploitative femininity, because it lacks the actual shouting, direct sexism, or overt racism of its more obvious (male) counterparts. Ironically, this loophole permits women to manipulate for personal gain the very system that constrains them. Thus, corporate culture creates a cycle that both supports and further embeds exploitative femininity.

In many senses, corporate culture's fixation on the strategic and an unwillingness to engage with the human element is counter-productive. It is, admittedly, uncomfortable for an organization to prioritize open and honest conversations over data-driven (sometimes superficial) analysis. There's no dearth of good writing around the transformation of corporate culture, but management and HR departments often choose shortcuts to create an illusion of progress.

Acknowledging that it is their very own culture and processes (rather than individual human behaviour) that allow exploitative femininity and other toxic behaviours to become entrenched is simply too difficult for many organizations. It's squishy and uncomfortable to address how people are actually treated within the workplace, how new colleagues are welcomed (or not), and how bystanders and reporters are perceived when issues arise. It's painful to realize that the same 'good girl' figures in multiple situations. It's hard to admit that existing processes that impact how seriously complaints are taken, the undermining of victims and an environment that discourages elevating issues to management and/or Human Resources are doing real harm, not just to individuals but to the organization itself. So, most companies focus on outcomes: easily quantifiable events or trends including a difficulty in retaining Black women at higher managerial levels, or at all. It's all well and good to see this, to count the talented lost professionals as they walk out of the door, but it doesn't solve the problem.

We as a universe of human professionals know how to do this better, but it's hard. Corporations must work towards a more introspective culture, even when the truth hurts. Organizations need to focus on the source of problems rather than simply documenting the outcomes. Destructive behaviours, most especially exploitative femininity, thrive in the rich soil of patriarchy and racism, and are fertilized by a corporate culture that looks the other way.

Exploring and understanding the foundations of a power structure and the way they shape our work environment is critical to creating a more equitable and productive workplace for all.

Yet, there is still one more blind spot that can in many ways be the most dangerous of all.

Women's employee resource groups

Until very recently, the role of many women's employee resource groups was to allow women to get together and talk about women's issues (before the role men play in gender equality was common knowledge). Many women joined these groups thinking they were a place to share sisterhood issues. Black women especially hoped to find a safe haven in which to discuss the experience of being a Black woman in the workplace, assuming that all women would be receptive to the entrenched challenges. The opposite was often true and the myth of sisterhood, as discussed at the beginning of this chapter, was exposed.

In too many cases, women's employee resource groups functioned as hunting grounds for a manipulator planning her next attack of exploitative femininity. What better place for the 'good girl' to position herself as a mentor, 'friend' or buffer between an uncertain colleague and the power network? In a women's group, the 'good girl' had access to the concerns, complaints and insecurities of other women, especially marginalized women (like the lone Black colleague). In addition to intelligence gathering, the manipulator also worked to silence the voice of her chosen victim, by assigning herself the role of a barrier between her mark and the rest of the group and the organization as a whole.

Because these groups were traditionally open only to women, the behaviour and gyrations of those who would use the confidences exposed in meetings for personal gain were hidden from management and Human Resources. Generally, these groups would not have the authority to effect strategic changes in the company even if (lacking a definitive structure or specified goal) they were able to identify and coalesce around changes the members would like to see.

Unfortunately, a savvy manipulator could still use her participation or leadership role in a women's employee resource group to portray herself as the expert and the best conduit to her more powerful network of 'what women really think'. Assuming this role allowed her to target individual colleagues, exert disproportionate influence on corporate policy and amplify her reputation as the indispensable, perfect female employee.

Effectively, her toxic behaviour was both compounded and even more hidden: exactly the opposite of what the well-intentioned creation of a women's group was designed to address.

Given how this behaviour flies under the radar and is supported, self-defence becomes even more critical. Let's see how you can help to dismantle this behaviour irrespective of your role in the situation.

Why is exploitative femininity especially damaging to Black women?

Companies the world over are trying to understand what they can do to retain Black women in their workforce. While this topic lends itself to its own, much more detailed book, this is a starting point.

An abundance of research demonstrates that Black women often feel isolated and unsupported in the workplace. This has been most recently confirmed during the COVID-19 pandemic, when

Black women felt more comfortable working from home because they were able to avoid the all-too-familiar microaggressions they faced in the office.

Despite so much research, two key questions are generally ignored: what does it feel like and what does it mean to walk into an office as a Black woman? Being the new woman in the office brings its own burdens, but being the only Black woman exacerbates the need to belong and to fit in.

The hurdles that Black women have to overcome in any workplace are many and add to the difficulty of trying to fit in while simultaneously working hard to push back against stereotypes. Whether it is being viewed as cold because a Black woman maintains a protective distance, or having to work against presumed questionable credibility, she also faces the extra burden of being unusually visible and especially scrutinized. If she joins the organization in a senior position or is promoted to a senior position, the challenges to a Black woman's authority are even greater than for women in general.

Having a friend or an ally goes a long way to alleviating an already stressful situation and this is where the 'good girl' – the exploiter we've already discussed – does the most damage. She understands this dynamic perfectly and uses her advantage freely. 'Good girls' are very clever at exploiting the uncertainty experienced by Black women in a work environment. Remember that the manipulative 'good girl' will be the first to invite her new colleague for coffee or lunch. At the beginning, she will provide the safety and comfort that is needed. She will also understand and be well versed in the problems Black women face, how much longer it takes to build relationships and how much more difficult it can be for people to vouch for Black women, so in many cases (abetted by her skills in deception) she will be difficult to spot and root out.

Most Human Resources processes make it difficult enough for any woman to make a complaint without it being traumatic. When a Black woman is involved, the process is even worse. The 'good girl' understands the role of racism and embedded stereotypes. She knows how the stereotypes provide people with comfort that their beliefs are correct, and she has no shame in exploiting that. The 'aggressive Black woman' trope is an ideal scapegoat, and along with her weaponized tears the 'good girl' ensures that Human Resources and management are on her side before speaking with a Black woman.

Add to this the fact that Black women generally receive the least managerial support and that they are the least likely to have sponsors within the organization. The isolation that the 'good girl' creates through her exploitative behaviour easily becomes the death knell for her victim's professional wellbeing and advancement possibilities.

We must acknowledge (and act upon) the fact that the damage done is greater than hurting an individual Black female colleague. The exploitation and its effects reinforce a wider rhetoric, one that affects the hiring of other Black women because the story becomes part of two detrimental, related narratives: (1) that 'We tried to hire Black women and it didn't work', and (2) that 'We hired a Black woman once and she was a bully'.

Both of these narratives will provide the justification that some organizations and/or managers seek to avoid hiring Black women. It also prevents organizations from digging deeper into the situation and rooting out the exploitative femininity that underlies the harm.

In a vicious cycle, the Black women stereotype provides the perfect cover for the 'good girl' because she knows that most grievances brought by Black women are ignored. Left unchecked, this 'good girl' might at some point be the source of a lawsuit against the company, but she also understands the world at large. Since Black women stand at the back of the queue, she knows the chances are high that she will get away with her exploitative behaviour.

The likelihood that she can do damage to generations of Black women is substantial, and for this reason it is critical that this behaviour is not only seen but that an active stand is taken against it.

Courageous leadership and exploitative femininity

Corrective strategies

Warning: exploitative femininity lurks within your workplace. You may be unaware of its presence, underestimate the damage it does, or even unwittingly create the circumstances in which it requires to thrive. This guide will help you recognize exploitative femininity, and develop strategies to defuse it and create a healthier work culture and more productive and equitable professional environment.

Exploitative femininity, like any form of manipulative behaviour, is harmful to the corporate setting, undermining a healthy, diverse and inclusionary space. It shatters careers, destroys collegiality and leaves residual feelings of guilt, fear and distrust. None of this makes your department or organization capable of its best work. Dissatisfaction limits productivity; teamwork suffers; staff turnover may be high – and all of this reflects poorly on you.

Your job involves detective work in order to identify the exploiter. This is often harder than it sounds because she has probably manipulated you as well as her colleagues, creating a nuanced (but false) illusion of reality to hide her abusive behaviour. To interrupt the pattern of damage, you will need time, a commitment to transparency, responsible protocols and a sound strategy.

The first step is to realize how unlikely it is that you will be able to change the behaviour of the exploiter. She has invested time and skill in creating a persona that facilitates her abuse and will go to great lengths to protect her advantage. She has cultivated an aura of victimhood. You, as well as her colleagues, have been a target of this deception. Managing this dynamic will require a degree of humility in acknowledging this fact before you can effectively root out and deal with the offender. If your knee-jerk reaction to the exploitative employee is to protect or defend her, you must honestly analyze why you believe that she is the one who is constantly bullied. If there are tears, steel yourself and stick to the evidence and your commitment to improving your workplace.

Establishing her credentials as the 'good girl' requires the (witting or unwitting) co-operation of people in power within the organization. She has built a network that might include the head of Human Resources, a managing partner, or your boss's boss. At least some of these people probably think she is indispensable, so unseating her will be a challenge. Your actions will require advanced planning so as not to further her narrative of victimhood. The danger here is magnified if you are a man. Keep in mind that it may be counterintuitive to some that removing a woman from a position of power is ultimately helpful in creating an inclusionary and gender-balanced workplace, and plan accordingly.

Your strategic plan will require transparency. Do not create a situation of trust with the offender you have identified or suspect. There can be no off-the-record conversations (which will undoubtedly be misreported and used against you). Strict protocols regarding scheduling and documenting meetings with her must be followed to avoid 'he said, she said' situations and even the perception of kinship or collusion. Dismantling exploitative femininity demands verified accounts of damaging behaviour, witnesses who can tell their own story and have not been groomed or primed by the manipulator and an avoidance of perpetuating gossip or commonly held assumptions that may not be fact-based.

An environment of almost judicial neutrality will serve you well. Process matters. A small committee may be useful to analyze and interpret the facts you have gathered from individuals. Decisions that flow from this process need to be evidence-based rather than anecdotal. Be prepared to question the underlying dynamic within your workplace rather than accepting at face value what your suspect claims. Assess character verifications (and assassinations) with an eye towards who stands to benefit, progress professionally within the organization, or grasp power. None of this will be quick and easy, but you and your entire staff deserve a culture of trust and co-operation, which requires surgical excision of exploitative femininity and any other form of manipulation or abuse.

Even as you read this, you might feel that the description of this behaviour is extreme, but remember this is all part of the manipulation. Viewing it as benign makes you less likely to take action, to make it something to be sorted out among colleagues, but this is where the courageous part of leadership comes in.

Being a leader is never easy. Guiding and leading your team through choppy waters is challenging for anyone. This is a moment when you will have to stand up against the crowd and dare to act differently to ensure that your company's culture can prosper and elevate. A leader putting gender equity into practice is vital as much on a team basis as it is on an individual one, ensuring that your team delivers, but also that you guide them to success. This is where the promotion process is crucial to driving gender equity.

Promotion

The purpose of a promotion is to acknowledge and reward an individual's contributions, expertise and potential for further advancement within an organization. Promotions typically involve an increase in job responsibilities, authority and/ or compensation, and are meant to recognize an individual's progress and development within the organization.

In general, promotions serve one or several of the functions listed below:

- Recognizing and rewarding hard work and contributions: promotions can help to acknowledge and reward an individual's hard work, expertise and contributions to the organization.
- Encouraging career development and growth: promotions can provide opportunities for individuals to take on new challenges, learn new skills and advance their careers.
- Supporting succession planning: promotions can help organizations identify and develop future leaders and ensure that there is a pipeline of talent ready to take on key roles as they become available.

- Demonstrating commitment to diversity, equity and inclusion: by promoting a diverse group of individuals, organizations can demonstrate their commitment to diversity and inclusion and create a more inclusive culture.

When Black women are promoted solely for the purpose of increasing diversity, it can create the perception that they were not truly qualified for the role and were only promoted because of their identity. This can lead to feelings of mistrust and resentment among employees, as well as a lack of confidence in the promotion process.

To avoid this, it is important for organizations to be transparent about their promotion criteria for everyone. With feelings of mistrust rife within the organization, the lack of transparency leads to heightened scrutiny, not just of the process, but also of the quality of her work.

It should not be the burden of a Black woman to be put in a position where she has to face questions about her authority and credibility because she has been deservedly promoted.

Similar to the role of a sponsor, it is also the role of your organization to provide her with that protection. Without transparency in process for everyone, her promotion will simply be for the sake of it and will also mean that she will have to expend energy in justifying her position and be locked in emotional battles, which will have an impact on her work. If she is under too much stress to deliver, this will feed into the narrative that she was not ready to take on the added responsibility, when the truth is quite different.

A promotion in responsibilities for many Black women means landing in a political position that they are ill-equipped to face.

The source of the politics is having to deal with the resentment of her colleagues.

Just as with workplace gossip, resentment can be very obstructive to her path of success.

The importance of equity within the promotion process is critical to create pathways for further generations of Black women who will join your organization. It's creating the governance that drives equity within the promotion process.

The barriers that Black women have historically faced and continue to face in the workplace due to racism and sexism have led to the following:

- Lack of representation in leadership positions: Black women are often under-represented in leadership positions, which can make it more difficult for them to be considered for promotions.
- Stereotyping and assumption: Black women face stereotyping in the promotion process, which can lead to their qualifications and achievements being overlooked or underestimated.
- Limited access to networking and mentorship opportunities: Black women may have less access to networking and mentorship opportunities, which impacts their visibility and chances of being considered for promotions.

Concrete ceiling: the 'concrete ceiling' refers to the invisible barrier that can prevent Black women and women of colour from advancing to top leadership positions. It was given this name to acknowledge how much harder it is to push through the ceiling due to both gender and race.

I am by no means saying that Black women in your organization should not be promoted, but, like the whole theme of this book, the promotion process should be viewed through a gender equity lens. Being meaningful in your approach and looking at both the results and the unintended consequences, both good and bad, is what will differentiate your organization from others in the future.

How have we reached this point? How can we mitigate the potential that her promotion is tokenistic?

Looking at the four factors that have influenced Black women being hindered from progressing, it comes back to the construction of the workplace.

If White men are determining promotion criteria, there is a risk that the criteria will be skewed and not reflective of the experiences, skills and qualifications of Black women. This can lead to Black women being passed over for promotions or not being given equal consideration for advancement.

There are a few potential effects of White men determining promotion criteria:

- Disparate impact on Black women: with skewed criteria, Black women will be less likely to be considered for promotions, which can result in a lack of representation in leadership positions.
- Lack of trust in the promotion process: if Black women feel that the promotion criteria are not fair or objective, they may lose trust in the promotion process and may be less motivated to pursue advancement opportunities, which further decreases the chances of building a Black female pipeline.
- Negative impact on organizational culture: homogenous leadership engenders further homogeneity. Affinity bias drives a lack of diversity in leadership positions, which further creates a culture that is not inclusive or welcoming to Black women.

Power is not the same as success.

This point is crucial in understanding the issues around meritocracy and why the best person doesn't always make it into the room. Those in power create the opportunities and those who have less power must fight to be seen.

Those who sit at the bottom of the power pyramid wield no power and influence over those at the top, but one of the most powerful assets they bring to the table is lived experience and this underscores the need for there to be a seat at the decision-making table across the whole structure if the aim of the game is to deliver on diversity targets, whether that is gender, race or sexuality.

Transparency becomes of the utmost importance as it allows the existing criteria to be challenged and discussed.

Some ideas for a transparent promotion process are:

- Clear criteria: the promotion criteria should be clearly defined and communicated to all employees. This can include qualifications, experience, skills and performance metrics that will be used to evaluate candidates for promotion.

- Diverse criteria committee: the criteria committee should be diverse and representative of the organization's workforce and across all levels of seniority. This can help to highlight barriers from different standpoints and ensure that all candidates are given equal consideration.

- Open communication: the promotion process should be open and transparent, with clear communication about the status and progress of each candidate. This can help to ensure that all employees feel informed and involved in the process.

- Feedback and support: candidates should be given feedback on their performance and provided with support to help them succeed in the promotion process. This can include access to training and development opportunities and guidance from mentors or sponsors.

- Regular review and evaluation: the promotion process should be regularly reviewed and evaluated to ensure that it is fair and inclusive. This can include gathering feedback from employees and adjusting as needed to improve the process.

As organizations build very specific targets around increasing representation of both women and Black women within their organization, the focus is on the outcome and output of reaching set targets as opposed to looking at the barriers that have previously prevented Black women from being promoted. Education on intersectionality and its impact in the workplace is important because it puts the focus on equity by acknowledging the different challenges Black women face due to their race and gender.

Intersectionality refers to the ways in which different aspects of a person's identity, such as their race, gender, class and sexual orientation, intersect and can create unique experiences and challenges.

There is another type of 'promotion' that causes resentment. I touched on this topic when it came to exploiting Black women's ambitions, but let's explore it further.

Exposure

Although exposure is not a traditional promotion, it is still viewed as such by many. In the position of being a representative, it often comes with access to senior rooms, with the possibility of attending events and the increase of internal value within many new circles. Whether she is the first Black woman or the only Black woman in a role or she is leading an initiative, her being acknowledged as a Black woman might make others feel not just uncomfortable but jealous, too.

This type of 'promotion' can be the motivation for some colleagues to get involved with the same initiatives as Black women in pursuit of getting the same exposure. In the case of DEI initiatives, this can be extremely dangerous because it can damage the work that has been done so far and inhibit significant cultural change.

Without providing organization-specific evidence that there are benefits to putting equity into practice, the focus on increased representation feels performative but also exclusionary by those who feel overlooked for opportunity. Instead of closing knowledge gaps around institutional and systemic barriers, exposure alone can serve as a source of resentment, in turn compounding the view that Black women get exposure based purely on their race and gender rather than expertise.

CHAPTER SIX

The Impact of Inaction on Black Women

It's important to recognize that the experiences and perspectives of Black women in the workplace are unique and often shaped by historical and societal factors, such as discrimination and bias. Focusing on equity, rather than equality, in the workplace can help to address these issues and create a more inclusive and equitable environment for all employees. This can include implementing policies and practices that support the advancement of Black women, as well as actively seeking out their input and perspectives. Additionally, it is important to recognize that the impact of discrimination and bias goes beyond the individual employee and affects the overall success and resilience of the organization. By taking an ecosystem view (meaning to see all the parts of a situation, impact and consequences both intended and unintended) and seeing each employee as a complete person, organizations can work towards creating positive outcomes and long-term impact.

This chapter is not intended to position Black women as being weak or being the problem, but to add context to the situation. There are outcomes and there is impact and while the desire is to create positive outcomes and impact, the damage that can be done by not taking an ecosystem view to gender equity risks undoing progress.

In the past two years it has become clear that organizations cannot continue to look at things through the binary lens of the employee and the person who they are outside, as they are the same person in different settings. We have also all been conditioned to believe that we are two separate people, but we are all now demanding to be seen as a single, complete person.

The concept of separate identities is the reason why so many organizations were surprised by the reverberations within the workplace following George Floyd's murder. There may have been a colour-blind approach, but in that pivotal moment many realized that they had Black employees and this spurred on movement focused on racial equity. Companies realized that spending so much time working means that a Black woman needs to be able to bring as much of herself to work as she chooses and that she needs to be valued and to feel engaged and protected.

The 2022[1] Edelman Trust Barometer, a yearly trust and credibility survey, established that societal leadership is now a core function of business and when this is viewed through the lens of gender equity it means that businesses now need to be prepared to speak and take action on issues such as race as well as gender.

The role of an employer is to understand the impact of societal burdens and to put them within the workplace context in building policies and processes that alleviate them.

Without the protective umbrella that is a company's brand, Black women have to deal with racism, sexism, misogyny and microaggressions. When I refer to the umbrella of a company's brand, Black women are afforded a certain level of protection

---

[1]https://www.edelman.com/trust/2022-trust-barometer

when they are working in comparison with a Black woman on the street. How she will be treated as an affiliate of your organization will make a difference, but it cannot protect her completely.

When she is outside the umbrella of your organization, her experiences are not commensurate with her position within it. Her educational calibre cannot be seen from the outside, nor her achievements, and it should not matter. But why does it?

Her social value is determined by stereotypes and the basis of others' assumptions who allow her gender and race to be the benchmark of her capacity, but what effect does corporate culture have on her social identity?

Social identity, that part of an individual's self-concept derived from membership of a relevant group, is situationally defined, as mentioned earlier in the book.

The idea that we have a work persona and a home persona is rooted in the influence of context. Depending on where we fall within the power spectrum, our identity in the workplace versus our identity in non-work settings can differ greatly. Black women, in particular, face a significant divergence between their work and social identities. The corporate world often fails to recognize or appreciate their true value, which has led many Black women to turn to side hustles. These side ventures allow them to express their personal worth without being constrained by a corporate culture that perpetuates patriarchy, racism, sexism and misogyny.

Corporate culture is not simply a static backdrop against which employees operate – it actively shapes and influences social identities. If a company's culture is not aligned with the identities of its employees, it can create significant challenges and even harm. For instance, if a Black woman is forced to behave inauthentically to fit a preconceived stereotype applied to her, it can be demoralizing and cause her to feel she does not belong in that environment. This is particularly true if she has to go to great lengths to conform to cultural expectations, such as carefully selecting her clothing so as to avoid being accused of being too provocative or worrying about whether her hairstyle is deemed 'professional' enough.

While all employees must make some adjustments to fit within the corporate culture, Black women often have to do more than most. They may feel a sense of pressure to conform to cultural norms that do not reflect their true selves or values, which can be emotionally taxing and affect their job performance. This is known as the 'double bind' – a phenomenon in which an individual is caught between conflicting expectations and cannot meet both.

These considerations are all extra burdens that a Black woman must carry just for being herself, but which she accepts because she makes sure she is qualified and competent and contributes above and beyond her job, so that she can eventually progress.

She tries to actively disprove stereotypes and any assumptions that her managers and colleagues may have. She is then on a gruelling schedule to do this. She's the first in the office. She's managing more projects than anyone else. She's answering all the emails, she's volunteering to chair committees, she's organizing client outings, she's organizing team outings and, on top of all of that, she is doing her day job. She understands the mechanisms of the workplace and that there are no second chances for Black women, so she pushes through. Then she will be recognized as being capable, a team player, collaborative and easy to work with, willing to volunteer – all factors that should make it easier for her to ascend the career ladder without issues.

Yet, even when she plays by the rules and is amenable and displays the characteristics mentioned earlier, she is seldom rewarded with recognition for her efforts.

Reward does not always have to be in monetary terms, although that is helpful. Take the factors that affect Black women being promoted, and the lack of access to networking or sponsorship/mentorship opportunities. Reward can also come in the form of providing the necessary access to senior members of staff or to leadership development programmes with an outcome of a new role to grow into.

Without any type of reward, she becomes despondent as she realizes that her 'above and beyond' performance is being taken for granted. Two things can happen, both of which lead to the same outcome.

Without recognition, she may slowly back down to a more sustainable (and appropriate) 100 per cent effort level, still easily meeting the requirements of the position. At some point, the manager and employee meet to discuss the reasons for an apparent drop-off in her productivity and contribution.

This is where the disconnect shows. Management tends to begin this conversation by questioning the employee's commitment to the company, possibly accusing her of lacking necessary focus, and doubting her ability to progress within the company. This stance acts as the beginning of a downward spiral in which trust, motivation and reward are on the table. On both sides, misunderstanding and expectations become entangled, with neither party satisfied and no constructive plan for nurturing a rewarding relationship between the firm and the employee going forward.

Fundamentally, the manager sees a staff member not meeting the impossibly high bar she has set for herself rather than judging her performance against the expectations communicated upon hiring her or the specific job description. The employee, on the other hand, may well feel overlooked and diminished because her overachievement has been ignored, sapping her initial motivation. There may also be issues with colleagues; she may be a victim of exploitative femininity; there may be external factors affecting her job. By beginning the conversation with accusations, though, the manager has blocked honest conversation regarding the root of what he sees as a problem. By not being able to acknowledge the employee's performance level as a manifestation of her dissatisfaction and a clear symptom of a situation that requires further exploration, the problem is further compounded.

She becomes disillusioned, which ultimately has the damaging effect of leaving her demoralized and unmotivated and unable to fully connect not just with her job but with her colleagues and with her managers.

This is the start of a vicious cycle, which begins with a lack of motivation that can lead to preventable mistakes, which leads to chastisement from a manager, which then leads to even more despondency, the feeling of unfair chastisement and isolation, which leads to even more preventable mistakes. Ultimately, the star of the team now becomes a burden on the team.

Her past performance of consistent delivery is not taken into consideration, nor is it recognized that she is not her usual self. Instead, she is now portrayed as someone who has inconsistently delivered.

This is usually the point of a critical breakdown in communication. How has it come to this?

Corporate culture traditionally teaches us to focus on specific behaviours without encouraging an exploration of context.

Comparable to parenting advice to focus on behaviours without addressing underlying issues, corporate reaction to dissatisfied employees has traditionally failed to distinguish between fleeting behaviours and those that signify more important issues, become ingrained and have broader, longer-lasting effects. It's more about a quick cure than thoughtful prevention and efforts to build a healthy environment.

At the point where it should be clear that there are bigger issues at play, the focus instead turns on whether she is a 'cultural fit' or a 'team player' and whether she is committed enough to the organization among her team and her managers.

These types of situations make Black women question if they should stay in organizations when consistent delivery is not enough to bring promotion, where, despite best efforts and being competent and willing to work hard, they are still overlooked and the only merit that has any value is the ability to fit in, in ways that she cannot because of her gender and her race.

In 2022, reporting on the experiences of Black women in the workplace was non-stop. Black women in the workplace were disproportionately suffering from burnout, having to manage racism and having no outlet for their stress in a professional setting.

The reality is that there is no other demographic of women that has the trope of being strong. The 'strong Black woman' trope has it that Black women are inherently strong and capable of handling any challenge or adversity they face. While this stereotype may seem positive on the surface, it can actually be damaging and harmful to Black women in a number of ways.

One impact of the strong Black woman trope is that it places unrealistic and unfair expectations on Black women to be constantly strong and resilient, even in the face of discrimination, oppression and other challenges. This can lead to feeling inadequate and overwhelmed, as Black women may feel pressure to constantly perform and meet these expectations.

Additionally, the strong Black woman trope can reinforce harmful stereotypes about Black women and their capabilities. By suggesting that Black women are inherently strong and capable, it implies that those who are not able to meet these expectations are somehow lacking or inferior. This can lead to further marginalization and discrimination.

Finally, where this trope can be at its most damaging is when it discourages Black women from seeking support or help when they need it. By reinforcing the idea that Black women should be able to handle everything on their own, it can create an environment where Black women feel that they cannot ask for help, seek support or make complaints when they need to. This can have a negative impact on their physical and mental health and wellbeing.

This further complicates any situation in which she is expected to respond to unfair treatment. With her femininity and vulnerability not being taken seriously, if she dares to express that side herself, then she risks being labelled as erratic.

This puts her between a rock and a hard place. Where does she go from here, if no one is willing to take her contribution seriously and recognize her skill set and if she is also not in a position to defend herself without recrimination? The answer is she will exit the business.

To illustrate this point, I will take the complaints process as an example.

Making a complaint at work is a difficult and nuanced decision for anyone, and especially so for Black women. There is much to consider, especially if she would like to stay at the company and progress in her career.

All too often for Black women, the outcome of filing an official complaint is looking for a new job in the long term. The short-term effect is commonly to become a professional outcast.

Black women do not have the luxury of being judged as individuals. They are very much aware that each decision they make affects not just them personally, but also the possibilities for other Black women who come after them.

In making a complaint, the overarching question is often: 'How will this tarnish my reputation, and am I ready to deal with the worst-case scenario, which may be looking for another job?'

One of the most widely held misconceptions surrounding this issue is that Black women make employment complaints just to 'cause trouble'. This is flatly an error of logic. A Black woman – in fact, any employee – complains in order to address and improve a situation, to make it possible for her to stay at the company and create positive outcomes for all involved.

Experiencing sexism and racism is exhausting at best and traumatizing at worst, but this often pales in comparison to the complaint process itself, where Black women (who are victims) are effectively put on trial.

Before she has even broached her complaint with HR, a Black woman has probably spent a long time trying to convince herself that the situation is not as bad as it seems, that she can survive this, and that it is easier or more useful to stay quiet than to be pigeonholed in the 'angry Black woman' box … and then to be punished by that label.

For most Black women, filing an official complaint can be career suicide. So how can companies make the process more productive and less retaliatory? For most employers, these elements of the complaint process demand attention:

- Who does a Black woman with an employment complaint have to speak to in HR?
- What is the corporate approach? Is it for Black women to prove their claims before action is taken, or are they assumed to be true and used as the basis for appropriate changes?
- How are Black women protected during the process? Are they asked to sit in a room with the offender to hear both sides of the story simultaneously, or can the intimidation factor be minimized with more careful and discreet HR policies?

Retaining and engaging with Black female talent requires a clear understanding that Black women are in a unique position and that companies have a responsibility to create solutions to the inherent inequities of the workplace. The following suggested solutions can help guide companies to improve their processes:

- Who does a Black woman with an employment complaint have to speak to in HR?

An obvious starting point is that the specific individual a Black woman speaks to in HR will dictate, or at least strongly influence within the structure of corporate policy, how the process unfolds.

Does the HR person understand what it is like to be a Black woman in the workplace, or are they on the defensive and already committed to siding with the company as opposed to listening to what they are being told? Is there someone in HR who specifically understands the unique position of Black women in the workplace?

Suggestion: at the very starting point of an employment complaint, companies should consider offering an external party to accept and discuss a complaint made by a Black female employee, so that she feels she has a safe place to talk and a neutral party to listen to her.

- What is the corporate approach? Is it for Black women to prove their claims before action is taken, or are they assumed to be true and used as the basis for appropriate changes?

Expecting a Black woman to prove that her reported experience is founded on racism and/or sexism undermines her credibility at the outset of the complaint process. Black women often face the challenge of being perceived as ill-equipped to understand the nuances of the workplace. It is critical that the processes in place do not compound this generally unfounded presumption. A company's understanding of the racist and sexist origins of inappropriate workplace behaviours and the frequency with which they occur makes it easier to eradicate them and create a more equitable environment.

Suggestion: companies should study their archives to see how many complaints by Black women have been successfully resolved. Assessing what was done well, and not so well, in the past can help inform necessary improvements. A record of few or no successfully resolved cases would it make abundantly clear that significant changes to the corporate approach are needed.

- How are Black women protected during the process? Are they asked to sit in a room with the offender to hear both sides of the story simultaneously, or can the intimidation factor be minimized with more careful and discreet HR policies?

In many complaints initiated by Black women, offending colleagues or supervisors attempt to 'front-run' the complaint. They hope to convince HR that they have done nothing wrong, and that the complaining employee is exaggerating or overly sensitive. This sort of intimidation and direct conflict with the object of a complaint is a primary driver of Black women's sense that employment complaints will be skewed to reflect poorly on them rather than inspiring action based on the true facts of the situation.

To counter this and to better protect the employment rights of Black women, companies must ensure confidentiality during the complaint process and require both parties to maintain public silence until the situation is resolved. Attempts to directly intimidate a complaining employee or else to garner support from potentially unrelated or uninformed colleagues does nothing to further impartial fact gathering and the imposition of appropriate measures to resolve the situation. Rather, these actions create even more conflict and diminish the likelihood of fair and successful outcomes.

Suggestion: to level the playing field of employment complaints, companies should assign each party a single confidant/e. These confidant/es should be registered with HR and be held equally responsible for keeping the situation confidential, with sanctions in place for breaking the rules.

In the world of criminal justice, the concept of restorative justice is used to describe the process when offender and victim meet. In most cases, this merely adds to the victim's trauma, especially when the offender does not truly regret his behaviour.

Bearing this in mind, companies should analyze their intentions in forcing face-to-face confrontation between a complaining employee and the person accused of harmful words and actions.

With intimidation strongly in play, are such meetings just another instance of Black women being expected to prove the facts that underlie their complaints, only for the accused to refute and deny the telling, or label it a misunderstanding?

Suggestion: if face-to-face meetings are part of a company's complaint process, HR must be very clear about the expected outcome. These meetings cannot be used as an opportunity to damage the credibility of an employee who lodges a complaint, to demonize or diminish Black women in general, or to undermine an individual's self-worth. These meetings are only useful if they can facilitate a resolution, and cannot be predicated on making the accused feel comfortable or vindicated at the expense of a colleague with legitimate complaints.

This example and the suggested solutions further emphasize why it is imperative that time, thought and resources are invested in identifying and eradicating the roots of workplace fairness problems. Without critical examination and a willingness to analyze the foundation and results of HR policies and practices, there will be no chance of closing the gap.

This is the initial impact of inaction, failing to retain Black women in your organization, but it goes further than that.

Every company has two reputations: the one they curate and control and the one that is discussed in private networks and informal communications channels.

While representation has the power to create the belief that an organization takes Black women and their ability to thrive seriously, there will still be conversations during which the cracks will show. As discussed earlier (*see* p. 56):

REPRESENTATION + CHANGE = POWER

Representation creates possibilities for younger and junior women to aspire to positions that they may not have otherwise aspired to, but younger Black women will also be looking at her position within the business critically. Does she seem empowered? Does she seem happy? Are Black women staying in their positions? If there is an exodus of Black women, and if so, why?

There is a secondary grapevine where most Black women in an organization are connected in some way. They may not be in each other's inner sanctums, but the most important messages are passed along. Are they safe in the organization and do they have opportunities to grow?

The future of organizations is Generation Z, so when representation is without power and change it comes across as disingenuous. Gen Z are characterized as being attracted to organizations that align with their values and are committed to making a positive impact on society. This can include organizations that prioritize sustainability, social justice, and diversity and inclusion. Gen Z may also value the opportunity to work for organizations that allow them to pursue their passions and make a meaningful contribution to the world and they are unafraid of holding organizations accountable, which can lead to the same outcome: finding other firms that are better aligned with their values and taking action in pursuing their goals.

The cost of inaction jeopardizes both the current and future workforce in a time when not only is it expected that organizations take a stand on social justice and racism and sexism, but organizations that still struggle to retain Black women will have a difficult time justifying this to stakeholders, whether they be board members, employees or customers.

Another emotional burden that Black women have to carry, as mentioned in Chapter 4, is that they have to wrestle with their feelings of being in a company that wants their face to indicate progress, but doesn't want to make the necessary changes. The organization dangles a carrot in front of them to say the more you do, the more we can give you, but up until now there's been more stick than carrot. This is where companies must tread carefully and understand their role in increasing the pressure in an already pressured situation.

There is a sense of urgency because as she is working even harder to find solutions, so the Black woman still believes and hopes that her organization will get it right. As she works harder, she is being pushed towards burnout.

The levels of burnout among Black women steadily increased during the pandemic but even pre-pandemic it wasn't news because all of these pressures have been present the whole time. The pandemic only exacerbated them and created more of a forum for them to be discussed, but it's been happening the whole time.

Suffering from burnout or mental health issues is something that is traditionally frowned upon within the Black community, which means that because of the strong Black woman trope it becomes difficult to ask for help; she doesn't want to be perceived as weak and personal issues or burnout often get taken into consideration when it comes to professional performance. For a lot of Black women, there is no professional comeback after burnout. Not because they don't want to come back, but because their colleagues and their employer do not know how 'to deal with them'. Human fallibility makes them feel awkward. They're tainted because the patriarchy does not allow for any femininity within its image of a Black woman: she is not allowed to be vulnerable. She's not allowed to be weak. She's not allowed to be tired and this defines part of the intersection of race and gender. That also fundamentally outlines why the experiences of Black women and White women are so radically different.

To be humanized and protected is the preserve of White women. To be seen as a workhorse, someone who executes and who is assertive, is the preserve of Black women. Which means there is no allowance for softness. There is no allowance for mistakes and it perpetuates the need for perfection and excellence because when there are only one or two Black women, every mistake they make is noted. It is remembered forever in her book of work within the company. Her performance will also be used as a barometer or benchmark for how other Black women will perform within the workplace.

The responsibility of the individual collective, which is the downside of representations, is another pressure as one person is expected to carry the reputation and the abilities of all other Black women who may potentially encounter them or follow them into the business base.

How can you recognize that there might be a problem of the individual collective in your business? Well, how many times to do people in your organization mix up two Black women?

It sounds trivial, but it speaks to the point, that when they are no longer individuals but are easily exchanged for another Black woman, there is no care being taken in getting to know them. This is a clear indication that there is a lack of understanding and empathy towards Black women in the organization, and that they are not being seen as individuals with their own unique experiences and perspectives.

At the foundation of gender equity is understanding what the barriers are for Black women that are not only within an organization. Black women are being penalized too for daring to be ambitious and those who are uncomfortable with their ambition also have the power to stop progress and are concerned with unfair advantages that are being freely given.

It is not enough just to focus on women, however, without looking at the intersection of gender and race, too. Gender equity has to be one of the foundational pillars of any diversity, equity and inclusion strategy.

CHAPTER SEVEN

Impact Due to Scarcity

What is a scarcity mindset and what exactly does it have to do with the workplace?

The scarcity mindset refers to a belief that resources, opportunities and success are limited and that there is not enough to go round. This mindset can lead individuals to focus on competition and hoarding resources, rather than collaboration and sharing.

The scarcity mindset can be driven by a variety of factors, including past experiences of scarcity, a lack of access to resources and societal messages about competition and success. It can also be fuelled by feelings of fear and insecurity, as individuals may feel that they must constantly strive to protect and accumulate resources in order to survive.

The scarcity mindset can have negative consequences, as it can lead individuals to focus on their own needs and interests at the expense of others. It can also create a competitive and stressful environment, as individuals may feel pressure to constantly perform and succeed in order to secure future resources and opportunities.

The fallout due to scarcity is huge and damaging. There are two elements to this. Scarcity breeds a scarcity mindset, which engenders discord in situations where there are few Black women within the business or across leadership.

Organizations end up pitting Black women against each other, usually by promoting one Black woman at the expense of others, or creating a competitive or hostile work environment where Black women are encouraged to undermine or sabotage each other.

Pitting Black women against each other can have negative consequences both for the individuals involved and the organization as a whole. On an individual level, it creates resentment, bitterness and isolation and, if allowed to, can also lead to a lack of trust and collaboration among Black women, which can hinder team effectiveness and productivity.

It should not be forgotten that there is also an impact on an organizational level, as pitting Black women against each other can create a toxic work environment that affects more than just the women involved, but also their teams. It can also hinder both of their career chances if they are also accused of creating a toxic environment.

The truth is that they are reacting to a situation that they have been placed in, rather than one they have created themselves.

In an environment of scarcity, the company has shown Black women that there is not enough space for more Black women to co-exist, so when a new Black woman joins an organization the implication is that she may be a replacement. This only applies in the same department, not across whole businesses.

One trend in the financial services sector is that Black women are often concentrated in back office and operational roles, rather than in front office positions such as client relationship management, portfolio management or product development. This can lead to a lack of representation and diversity in these more visible, high-profile roles. Additionally, when there is only a small number of Black women in an organization, they may be isolated and feel a lack of community within the company. This can further exacerbate the challenges they face and reinforce the idea that Black women are not capable of occupying a variety of roles across the business.

In the past two years, there is no doubt that the scope of roles for Black women has increased, but there is also no denying that many companies have been creative in finding solutions by making superficial changes that give the appearance of progress. This usually happens when they create new titles, which have no clarity of objectives and are a hotch-potch of several roles.

These types of roles do not create career paths or a sustainable pipeline, so two questions to ask are:

1) Have we created roles for Black women that offer paths and growth potential within the business?

2) Can we build a team and infrastructure around a Black woman to show that this role is embedded within the company's structure and that it won't disappear if she leaves the business?

The initial part of scarcity is quite clear. Scarcity mindset means fear; it creates fear in these women, which puts them in a position of always having to defend their position for fear of being replaced. There are still, however, companies, which I label high-pressure, that mistakenly subscribe to this mentality in general. They prioritize making their employees feel dispensable because they think that it will increase productivity.

As a mechanism of control, the scarcity mindset is meant to ensure that Black women give their best at all times, under all circumstances, because if they don't then there is another Black woman waiting in the wings – who is hungrier, who is even more prepared, who is more amenable to be told what to do and say in order to become successful within this company culture.

Scarcity combined with feelings of being dispensable drives the need and compunction to be a cultural fit, to blend in, to be invisible, to do everything to avoid being seen as a problem. If she raises concerns or issues, she can find herself unwittingly in a situation of psychological intimidation, where another Black woman is referred to as being a 'good citizen', to create instability. This allows space for constant pressure, even when nothing is said and also has the same effect of breeding contempt between two people who are experiencing the same oppressions within one system but are now competing and vying for attention. Instead of being collaborators, they have been forced into competition. The system of scarcity follows the principle of divide and conquer and can be deftly applied. It manipulates the concept that Black women cannot attain a certain standard, because who better to use a benchmark than another Black woman?

Who becomes the benchmark will depend on the desired outcome, but by creating competition and one successful outcome, the goal becomes: how can I be better than the benchmark? This may involve undermining the decisions and suggestions of the other person.

You might be wondering why these women would even begin to be involved in this.

The answer is so that they can succeed. They are forced to pick themselves and this means openly backing themselves for fear of being pushed out of a job. Each woman is no longer seen and valued for her individual contribution, but in comparison with another Black woman.

The system of scarcity also supports the positioning of being an intruder. It also indicates being tolerated rather than tolerance. There is a marked difference between the two. An intruder is designed, defined as being somebody who is in a place that they are not supposed to be in. Scarcity implicitly confirms that you are not supposed to be there because the choice has been made that there is only space for a few. All the reasons that organizations give as to why they cannot find Black female talent are further ways to circumnavigate putting in the hard work.

It is an uncomfortable truth, but it remains nonetheless. Equity and speed tend not to go hand-in-hand, so whether it is deliberate or not, by falling back on excuses, the scarcity system principle is being perpetuated, which erodes your chances of building an inclusive culture.

The scarcity system forces Black women into survival mode; they do not belong to the culture, but they are tolerated. They have to be hyperaware of any potential issues, as they recognize the precariousness of their position. The constant confirmation that they are tolerated means they have to be prepared for attacks or ways of being pushed out. They understand that the rules of the game are not being shared with the Black woman and that she should be expected to feel grateful for having access to this space.

The scarcity system is intertwined with racism and sexism and, without addressing both sources of oppression within the workplace, she will always remain an outsider.

The more senior you are, the fewer Black women there are, which suggests that the Black woman may be an anomaly.

The definition of an anomaly is 'something that deviates from what is standard, normal, or expected'.

Her presence will be publicly celebrated, but the 'Why is she here and how did she get here?' questions will continue to bubble beneath the surface.

Without building clear pathways within organizations that remove the barriers to entry for Black women into management positions, junior or otherwise, the ascent of Black women will forever seem anomalous rather than normal.

Increased representation within all levels of management dispels some of the notions that only a very small number of Black women are capable of achieving corporate success.

The scarcity mindset can thus have far-reaching and negative impacts on Black women and the culture of an organization. When an organization perpetuates a narrative of scarcity, it sends a message that there is a limited pool of talent and limited opportunities, which can create competition and undermine inclusivity.

This has negative consequences for Black women, as they will feel that they are not valued or that they must constantly compete for resources and opportunities. Additionally, the scarcity mindset can create a toxic work environment that is not supportive or collaborative, and which can hinder the success of all employees.

Being able recognize and challenge the scarcity mindset will increase awareness to enable a focus on abundance and collaboration, rather than competition. This is pivotal to creating a more supportive and inclusive environment in which Black women and all employees can thrive.

Representation

The power of representation can never be understated. Its goal in organizations is important in helping to ensure that the perspectives and experiences of diverse groups are reflected and taken into account in decision-making and policy-making. With the benefits ranging from showing that there are career possibilities to increased job satisfaction with having leaders who look like them, the potential is unlimited in improving culture.

However, there are also dangers to representation in organizations that can result in tokenism, rather than true inclusion and diversity.

One such danger is when there is no power along with the representation. Without power, representation can be used in a superficial way, where a few individuals from under-represented groups are promoted to leadership positions without being given the same opportunities, resources and support as their colleagues. The net result is that they are prevented from making meaningful changes to policies and practices.

In a 2021 US survey by the Gallup Center on Black Voices,[1] two things became clear. Firstly, representation positively impacts the experience of Black employees. But there is a problem: 62 per cent of respondents believed that the presence of Black leaders indicated that the organization would ensure that they were treated correctly.

This supports one of the dangers of representation: that it can create the expectation that individuals from under-represented groups should represent the interests and experiences of their entire group. This can lead to a burden of representation, where these individuals are expected to speak on behalf of their entire group and may feel pressure to conform to stereotypes or expectations.

---

[1] https://news.gallup.com/poll/328457/representation-shapes-black-employees-work-experience.aspx

The expectation combined with a lack of power can be a potent cocktail. Without the Black woman knowing that she is not in the position to create change, but assuming because of her seniority and involvement that she is a decision-maker, when change fails to materialize it leads to disillusionment not in the organization but in her. She begins to believe that she cannot fulfil a role with all the tools at her disposal.

She is also in a position of not being able to share where and how her hands are tied, so she must suffer in silence and on her own, which will slowly erode any credibility and reputation she has within her community.

There are two assumptions that we have to remove:

1) every Black female leader wants to be an advocate for gender equity or racial equity;
2) seniority automatically correlates to having decision-making power and influence on a broader scale.

Being the only one or being one of few puts many Black women in the position of being role models; yet not every Black woman wants to take up that role officially and the responsibility that comes with it. This is not a criticism, as it should be her right to decide if she wants to take up this baton, but it is an organization that determines whether or not her role is meaningful.

Meaningful in this context is how she will be able to positively impact the lives of other employees within the organization.

To achieve that she will need explicit support, which will come in the form of resources, participation in decision-making meetings and powers to execute those decisions in the way she sees fit.

From the perspective of an organization, the questions are:

- Have you asked her/them if they want to be involved in equity work or has it been heavily suggested as a good idea, with the line 'seeing as we are focusing more on diversity, equity and inclusion...'?
- Commitment means taking action: have you worked with her to build a strategy that focuses on making important changes or, rather, given her a plan that she needs to follow?

Being powerless in these situations can also mean being told what to do rather than being asked. Focusing on the bigger picture and not on her specific needs.

Habitually, we focus on Black women in leadership, but what about all the other Black women in your organization? There is an opportunity to accelerate gender equity on an individual level.

The question is: how can an organization allow each Black woman to feel empowered?

The power in the equation Representation + Power = Change does not have to mean that the person must have business-wide influence. The ability to be able to change her immediate surroundings is just as important as any governance. If each woman can show up as her authentic self, she will speak about how she reached that point. She will work not only as an evangelist for her manager, but for your organization, as space has been created for her to breathe and expand.

Gender equity in an organization is based on the collective experiences of individuals and how they shape the culture and policies of the organization. If their experiences do not shape the culture and policies, this is representation minus power, which is tokenistic.

This will be covered in the chapter on practical applications and our REASON framework, but this is why co-creation is so important, as it utilizes lived experience and expertise to ensure that the way the policies and processes are shaped is relevant for Black women in your organization.

Examining and addressing the specific experiences and challenges faced by Black women in the organization is the starting point in driving gender equity, alongside reading and learning from this book.

The benefits of Representation + Power = Change are improved morale, productivity and overall organizational success.

It's important to recognize that individual experiences and perceptions of Black women within an organization can have a significant impact on the organization's reputation in informal networks. This includes not only the experiences of Black women within the organization, but also how they are perceived and treated by their colleagues and managers and if there are consequences if it is discriminatory.

CHAPTER EIGHT

Challenges and Course Correction

While many organizations are recognizing the need to address issues of diversity, equity and inclusion (DEI) in the workplace, it is important to consider the specific challenges that Black women face. When organizations begin to address these issues, there are often unintended consequences that can minimize the impact of their efforts. This chapter will focus on these blind spots and provide guidance on how to correct them even if actions have already been taken.

First, this chapter will examine some of the well-intentioned actions that organizations take to address issues of DEI, and how these actions can create unintended consequences for Black women. This includes policies and programmes that fail to take into account the unique experiences and challenges that Black women face in the workplace.

Understanding the intersectionality creates the space to begin to learn about Black women's experiences. This includes recognizing that these are not only shaped by their race and gender, but also by other factors, such as socioeconomic status, education and sexual orientation.

Finally, this chapter will offer practical solutions for organizations to correct these blind spots, such as involving Black women in decision-making, providing support for professional development and career advancement, and creating a culture of inclusion and belonging for Black women.

Employee resource groups

Employee resource groups (ERGs) are often created with the intention of fostering a sense of belonging and community for under-represented groups in the workplace. However, a knee-jerk reaction to creating ERGs without specifically addressing the needs of Black women can lead to more damage being done than good.

Most organizations have either an ERG for Black people or an ERG for women, which makes it harder for Black women to feel that they fit in with other groups or that their experiences are fully understood or acknowledged. The double-edged sword for the Black woman is the expectation that she should be thankful that there is a space for her at all, so it discourages her from voicing her opinions, which can lead to the opposite effect, where she feels excluded, isolated and disillusioned.

The reality is that you may not have more than one Black women in your organization, so what can you then do?

You can adapt your approach. If there is not a large enough cohort, then look for an industry association or ask her if she knows of one, the membership of which can be paid for by the organization.

This is not to say that she cannot participate in a Women of Colour ERG, but to highlight the importance of her being able to share the specific challenges and experiences that Black women face in the workplace without fear of judgement and the need to explain more.

There are many ways that you and your organization can still provide support even if it requires external support.

If, however, you do have enough Black women in your organization and have created an ERG, what can you do to ensure that you have set them up for success? An ERG should run in much the same way as a business unit and should be viewed with the same level of seriousness, from the perspective of having objectives and purpose.

Here are some tips:

- Define the purpose and goals of the ERG: it is important to have a clear understanding of the purpose and goals of the ERG from the start. This will help to guide the group's activities and ensure that they are aligned with the organization's overall DEI goals.
- Identify key stakeholders and involve them in the planning process: identify key stakeholders, such as employees, leaders and other members of the organization, who can provide valuable input and support for the ERG. Involving these stakeholders in the planning process can help to ensure that the ERG is supported and has the resources it needs in order to be successful.
- Develop a governance structure: establish a clear governance structure for the ERG, including roles and responsibilities for members, leadership and sponsors. This will help to ensure that the ERG is well organized and that decision-making is transparent and inclusive.
- Create a plan for communication and outreach: develop a plan for communication and outreach that includes ways for the ERG to connect with its members, share information and updates and gather feedback. This can help to build a sense of community and engagement among members.
- Establish metrics to measure success: establish metrics to measure the success of the ERG, such as membership numbers, retention rates and engagement metrics. This will help to ensure that the ERG is meeting its goals and can be used to make necessary adjustments.

- Set up regular review and evaluation: it's important to regularly evaluate the ERG's performance, activities and impact and make adjustments accordingly. Review the group's effectiveness, share feedback and involve members in the process.
- Provide support, resources and training: provide the ERG with necessary resources such as budget, office space, communication tools and access to training and development opportunities. This will help to ensure that the ERG has the support it needs to be successful.

Another important point to consider is whether they have access to senior leaders. Is there also business alignment for their objectives and goals for the year? Is there a member of the senior leadership team who sponsors and advocates for the group?

When it comes to ERGs, having a senior sponsor who is committed to the group's mission and purpose is essential for its success. This sponsor may come from any demographic and does not necessarily have to be a Black woman. However, it is important that the sponsor is able to provide support and help build strategy for the group.

One important aspect of a sponsor's role is being hands-on and actively involved in the group's activities. This includes providing guidance and resources for the group to achieve its goals, and being a liaison between the group and leadership. A sponsor's involvement and support can also help to ensure that the group's voice is heard and that their recommendations and ideas are taken seriously by leadership.

Moreover, a sponsor should be aware of the intersectionality and nuances of the experiences of Black women and provide guidance accordingly. The sponsor should also have a deep understanding of the issues and barriers Black women face in the workplace and have the ability to translate that understanding into actionable strategies.

The sponsor should also be able to ensure that the ERG for Black women is not seen as a 'Band-Aid solution', but as a comprehensive and ongoing effort to improve the experience and representation of Black women in the organization.

For the ERG to serve its purpose, work in the best interests of Black women and be valued by your organization, Black women need to be involved in the design, development and implementation stages.

By taking these and other steps, your organization can work towards creating a more diverse and inclusive environment for all employees, including Black women.

Leadership development programmes for Black women

Leadership development programmes are a wonderful way of accelerating the careers of high-potential talent and also enhancing their skills, so that they can be a part of the future leadership team. They are also beneficial for both the individual and the organization.

The benefits are considerable, ranging from:

- Improving skills and knowledge: leadership development programmes typically provide employees with the opportunity to learn new skills and acquire knowledge that can help them become more effective leaders. This can include learning about leadership styles, decision-making, communication and problem-solving, among other things.
- Encouraging personal and professional growth: leadership development programmes can help employees to identify their strengths and weaknesses, as well as set and achieve personal and

professional goals. By participating in a leadership development programme, employees can gain a sense of direction and purpose and grow both personally and professionally.

- Building a culture of leadership: leadership development programmes can help organizations to create a culture of leadership by encouraging all employees to take an active role in shaping the organization's direction. This can help to create a sense of shared ownership and accountability among employees and can lead to increased engagement and productivity.

- Improving retention and recruitment: investing in leadership development can help organizations retain current employees and attract new ones. Employees who feel that they are being invested in and developed tend to be more satisfied and loyal to their organization, which can help to lower staff attrition.

- Improving overall organizational performance: when employees have the skills and knowledge they need to be effective leaders, organizations tend to perform better. Strong leaders can help to improve communication, collaboration and decision-making, which can lead to increased productivity, profitability and innovation.

- Diversifying the leadership pipeline: diversifying the leadership pipeline and training employees from diverse backgrounds can benefit organizations in multiple ways, including increasing innovation, improving customer satisfaction and increasing overall employee engagement.

The last point in this list is the one I would like to focus on.

Creating a Black women-only leadership development programme may seem like a logical solution to addressing the underrepresentation of Black women in leadership roles. However, it is important to acknowledge that this approach may not be the most effective way to support the advancement of Black women within an organization.

One of the main reasons why a Black women-only leadership development programme may not be effective is that it can perpetuate the notion that Black women need special treatment or support to succeed in the workplace. This can create a sense of othering (making someone feel like an alien because they are different from you) and can make Black women feel as if they are not fully accepted or valued within the organization.

Additionally, a Black women-only leadership development programme may not provide the same opportunities for networking, mentoring and exposure as a more inclusive programme would. It can also create segregation and can limit the exposure of the participant to the diverse perspective; it will also not help the women to adapt to the existing corporate structure and navigate the system that it is in place.

Another important aspect is that providing a separate leadership development programme for Black women may also not address the underlying issues, such as discrimination, bias and lack of sponsorship, that prevent Black women from advancing in the organization. Therefore, it may not be an effective solution to the problem of underrepresentation of Black women in leadership roles.

A more effective approach would be to address these underlying issues and systemic changes by incorporating leadership development modules on gender equity, racial equity and mentoring through a gender equity lens, coaching, providing stretch assignments (*see* pp. 149–150) and sponsorship, addressing the knowledge gaps and offering and normalizing these as part of the skill set of future leaders. By making these changes, your organization can create a more inclusive and equitable culture that supports the advancement of Black women and all employees from the top down.

An inclusive leadership development programme can also be beneficial for the organization as a whole, as diverse leaders are more likely to drive innovation and better decision-making. This will result in a more productive and successful organization overall.

Having one leadership development programme for the entire organization, rather than a separate one for Black women, can have several benefits. One of the main benefits is that it can help to educate other leaders within the organization about the barriers Black women face in the workplace. By raising awareness of these barriers, other leaders can become more equity-minded and better equipped to support the advancement of Black women within the organization.

If you have already created a leadership development programme, I would advise checking in with your cohort: how do they feel? Do they think they are being given the right tools? Has it been made clear that they are receiving preferential treatment? Do they feel that the programme is meeting their needs and that their provider understands their position? Would they prefer to be part of a general cohort and did they participate in this programme simply because it was offered?

Leadership development programmes that are viewed as a tick-box exercise tend to have a number of shortcomings, such as lack of follow-up and accountability, which diminishes the overall impact of the programme. A tick-box mentality towards leadership development can also make the programme lose its sense of purpose and not adequately address the unique challenges faced by certain groups, such as Black women.

An effective leadership development programme should be built around the specific needs and goals of the organization and tailored to the specific needs of the participants. The programme should be designed to align with the organization's culture and values, and provide opportunities for participants to put their new skills and knowledge into practice.

This also means that a Black woman should have a new role to grow into. It does not have to be immediately, but the quickest way for a programme to seem performative is if there is nowhere for her to progress. A new role does not have to mean a complete overhaul, but it should be a clear step forward from where she was. The parameters for when she can expect the jump to occur should also be clearly defined.

It is important for growth opportunities to be provided to individuals after they have participated in a leadership development programme. Without such opportunities, the learning and development gained from the programme may not be applied and the investment in the programme may not yield its intended results.

Providing growth opportunities after participating in a leadership development programme can help to solidify the new skills and knowledge gained and ensure that they are applied in the workplace. This can include stretch assignments, projects or additional responsibilities that allow the individual to put their new skills into practice and build their confidence.

These opportunities can also help to demonstrate the organization's commitment to the professional development of its employees, and can provide a sense of purpose, motivation and engagement, leading to a more productive workforce and a better return on investment for the company.

Furthermore, providing growth opportunities can help to address the issues of underrepresentation and advancement of Black women in leadership roles. Creating a clear pathway for Black women to advance and providing opportunities for leadership roles can help to increase representation and diversity within the leadership ranks.

CHAPTER NINE

The Crutch of Data and Requesting Self-identification

In 2022, there was a significant push for self-identification within organizations, as a way to gather data on the diversity of their workforces. However, marginalized and minoritized groups are often the least likely to want to contribute to this data, leading to organizations using the lack of data as a reason for not taking action on DEI issues. This use of data as a crutch for inaction is problematic because it suggests that organizations are more interested in collecting data than in actually taking steps to support and value these groups.

Self-identification can be a sensitive issue, especially for marginalized groups who may have experienced discrimination in the past. It is important for organizations to create a safe and comfortable environment in which employees can self-identify, and to ensure that the data collected will be used to inform and drive real change within the organization.

The push for self-identification can also be seen as a ransom for support, as organizations may use the lack of data as an excuse not to provide resources and support for marginalized and minoritized groups. This is problematic because it can create a lack of trust and a sense that the organization is not genuinely committed to DEI.

Instead of using anecdotal data, organizations should focus on proving that they value and support marginalized and minoritized groups. This can be done by taking tangible steps to address DEI issues, such as implementing DEI training for employees, creating employee resource groups and engaging in active listening and collaboration with marginalized and minoritized groups.

It is important for organizations to understand that self-identification data is just one piece of the puzzle; important but not enough. They need also to focus on creating an inclusive culture and environment, where employees feel valued and respected regardless of their background. Additionally, organizations should have a zero-tolerance policy for any discrimination, bias or exclusion.

Each organization's priority should be that the experiences of marginalized and minoritized groups are improved and that each organization demonstrates the value of self-identification for the individual rather than the organization.

Organizations need to be more transparent about how they plan to use data on employee diversity, especially when it comes to data on intersecting identities. Many marginalized and minoritized groups are hesitant about sharing this information if they don't know how it will be used, or if they don't trust the organization to use it in a responsible and ethical manner.

Being transparent about how data will be used can help to build trust with employees and make them more likely to share information on their identities. For example, organizations can share their data collection policies and explain how they plan to use the data, including who will have access to it and how it will be protected. They can also involve employees in the data collection process, by providing them with information on why the data is being collected, what it will be used for and how it will benefit them.

When it comes to data on intersecting identities, organizations need to be aware that individuals may face multiple forms of discrimination and marginalization based on their identities. Having more information on the many forms of intersecting identities can help organizations to better understand and address these issues.

For example, data on an employee's race, gender identity and sexual orientation can help organizations to identify patterns of discrimination and bias that may be impacting various groups differently. This information can then be used to inform DEI strategies and programmes, and ensure that they are more inclusive and effective.

In summary, organizations need to be more transparent about how they plan to use data on diversity and especially on intersecting identities. By doing so, they can build trust with employees, increase data collection and use it effectively to address discrimination and bias. Additionally, the data can help organizations to better understand and address the unique experiences and challenges faced by different groups of employees.

A personal data request also requires personal support. Asking employees for personal data can be a sensitive and emotional process, and it is important for organizations to provide personal support to employees who may be hesitant about sharing this information. This is especially true for marginalized and minoritized groups, such as Black women, who may have had negative experiences with sharing their personal information in the past.

It is also important to provide employees with the option not to share their personal data, and to respect their decision if they choose this path.

Personal support should not be withheld simply because organizations may not know exactly how many Black women are in the organization. The true value of support is ensuring that those who are present feel heard, valued and respected. Personal support can include activities such as providing a safe space for employees to share their experiences, offering counselling services and connecting employees with support groups or resources.

It is important for organizations to recognize that collecting personal data is a process that requires sensitivity, trust and mutual understanding.

Organizations should make sure that their managers and employees are trained in the importance of understanding intersectionality and how to handle sensitive conversations, and are able to provide a safe space for employees to share their data and experiences.

Building trust is a critical component of addressing DEI issues in the workplace, particularly when it comes to marginalized and minoritized groups like Black women. However, it can be challenging to build trust when organizations are primarily focused on collecting data before taking action to improve policies and processes.

One way to build trust with Black women is to focus on improving policies and processes without relying solely on data. This means taking concrete steps first. Doing this demonstrates a genuine commitment to DEI and creates a tangible sense of change, which can help to build trust.

Organizations have a responsibility of care to all their employees, including Black women. They should avoid treating Black women solely as a data set, and engage with them in meaningful ways and create opportunities for them to share their experiences and perspectives.

Stretch assignments

A stretch assignment is a task or project that is outside an individual's comfort zone and requires them to learn new skills or take on new responsibilities. These assignments are often given to employees as a way of challenging them and helping them grow professionally.

Stretch assignments can be a valuable learning opportunity for employees, as they allow them to develop new skills, build confidence and broaden their experience and expertise. These assignments can also benefit organizations, as they can help to develop the capabilities and potential of their employees.

Some examples of stretch assignments might include leading a team for the first time, working on a project outside an individual's area of expertise, or taking on a role with increased responsibility or visibility.

However, organizations must proceed with caution in avoiding packaging DEI work as a stretch assignment for Black women. It is vital to understand the difference between lived experience and expertise and the role you want her to stretch into. Volunteering to help support events is one thing, but taking an active role is very different.

Giving Black women DEI work as a stretch assignment task can be problematic for several reasons.

Firstly, DEI work can often be emotionally taxing and may require a significant amount of time and energy to be dedicated to it. Asking a Black woman to take on DEI work as a stretch assignment can put an additional burden on her and can be seen as the organization expecting them to 'fix' the problem of discrimination and bias within the workplace. This can create feelings of frustration and burnout for Black women.

Secondly, DEI work should not be seen as an add-on or 'extra' task, but, rather, as an integral part of every employee's role. Expecting Black women to take on DEI work as a stretch assignment implies that it is not everyone's responsibility and perpetuates the idea that only certain individuals should be responsible for promoting diversity and inclusion.

Thirdly, DEI work can be isolating. Black women can end up feeling like they are the only ones fighting for equity, and without proper support it can wear them down.

Fourthly, if the remit of this stretch assignment is not clearly defined or if performance expectations are unrealistic, she may struggle to meet them and may become discouraged, which further adds to the burdens she faces in the workplace.

Taking a fix-the-system approach

This is probably one of the hardest changes to achieve. It requires addressing problems or issues that seeks to change the underlying systems or structures that are causing the problem, rather than just treating the symptoms. The focus is on identifying and addressing the root causes of the problem, rather than just trying to alleviate the symptoms.

We automatically think of someone fitting into an organization's culture and when they don't, the organization either tries to change the person through 'constructive' feedback and sometimes penalization or by getting rid of them entirely.

We have been taught to accept cultural fit instead of cultural disruption. We have been taught to protect the system at all costs, which means that taking a fix-the-system approach puts us out of our comfort zone.

This is no different in the case of Black women. The common approach of organizations is trying to 'fix' Black women in order to address issues of discrimination and bias within the workplace. The 'fix' in this case is assimilation and a smoothing of the edges that make them stand out.

An attempt to fix Black women leads to a distraction from examining the corporate structure and its impact on Black women, highlighting how working hours, job and promotion criteria and access to resources are often designed, even if unintentionally, to keep them out.

Having a definitive narrative is crucial when it comes to addressing issues of discrimination and bias in the workplace, particularly as it relates to Black women. However, when not done properly it can perpetuate harmful stereotypes that position Black women as the problem and the intruder.

As will be discussed in the Chapter 13, the problems have to be looked at from the standpoint of 'what has prevented the progress of Black women to this space, when White men have no problems getting there?'

It is easier to blame the issues on Black women, as you can get rid of them. It is much harder to dismantle a system and a power structure that has been in place for centuries.

When looking at the system and your own position within the power structure, you will also start to analyze how you may have benefited from your position within the power structure, but that should not be your stopping point. The important part is: how can you use your position to amplify the voices of others within the organization?

The rise and relevance of ESG for gender equity

The rise and relevance of ESG for gender equity delves into the growing importance of ESG criteria for achieving gender equity in the workplace. The introduction of this chapter will provide an overview of the current state of gender equity in the workplace, the emergence of ESG as a key consideration for companies and the interlink between gender equity and sustainability. It will highlight the growing awareness among investors and consumers of the importance of gender equity in the business world, and how ESG considerations can be used to drive progress in this area. The chapter will examine the ways in which companies can integrate gender equity into their ESG strategies, and how this can lead to long-term financial and societal benefits. The chapter will also explore the challenges and barriers that companies may face in implementing gender equity and ESG initiatives, and the role of stakeholders in promoting progress. The introduction will set the stage for the in-depth examination of the rise and relevance of ESG for gender equity that will be presented in the rest of the chapter.

Environmental, social and governance factors were originally integrated as part of responsible investing that would drive better investment processes and decision-making. ESG factors have the ability to significantly impact the financial success of organizations. ESG criteria can be used to evaluate the performance of companies and their potential for long-term growth.

When it comes to environmental factors, companies that score well on measures such as carbon emissions, energy efficiency and use of renewable energy are seen as better positioned for long-term growth, as they are less exposed to the risks of climate change and better able to adapt to a low-carbon economy. Governments and regulators around the world are implementing policies to reduce greenhouse gas emissions and encourage the use of renewable energy, creating a credible business case for companies to improve their environmental performance.

On the social side, companies that prioritize labour rights, human rights and gender equity tend to have engaged employees, satisfied customers and supportive communities. This, in turn, can lead to long-term financial performance and stability. Companies that prioritize social factors also tend to have better risk management strategies in place, which can help them navigate challenges such as economic downturns and natural disasters.

Governance factors, such as transparency, accountability and corporate culture, are also critical to financial success. Companies with strong governance practices are more likely to be well managed, have a clear strategic direction and be responsive to the needs of all stakeholders. Good governance also helps to mitigate risks such as corruption and fraud, which can damage a company's reputation and financial performance.

However, *not* addressing ESG factors can have negative consequences for organizations. Companies that ignore environmental concerns may face increased regulatory scrutiny and penalties, as well as reputational damage. They may also face higher operating costs due to a lack of energy efficiency and a failure to invest in renewable energy. Companies that do not prioritize social factors such as labour rights and human rights may face fines, legal action and reputational damage. As much as implementing ESG strategies can benefit an organization, the impact of inaction can be equally severe, especially when or if 'purpose washing' is discovered.

Purpose washing is the practice of companies promoting their commitment to social and environmental causes, also known as 'greenwashing' or 'causewashing', without actually taking significant action to address these issues. This is often done to improve a company's reputation and appeal to socially conscious consumers without actually making meaningful changes to their business practices.

ESG factors will continue to significantly impact the financial success of organizations and there will be an increasing requirement that organizations prove they are taking action and being transparent about how they are prioritizing environmental, social and governance factors. Investors and stakeholders are becoming increasingly savvy and considering these factors when evaluating companies, and those that score well on ESG criteria may be seen as more attractive, whether as potential investment opportunities or as potential employers.

Historically, the predominant focus of ESG criteria was on environmental factors. This emphasis was driven by concerns about climate change and the need to transition to a more sustainable economy. Investors began to use ESG criteria to evaluate companies' environmental performance, such as their carbon emissions, energy efficiency and use of renewable energy. It is crucial to highlight that strategy also looks at long-term positioning and the impact of protecting the planet to secure our future. Companies that scored well on these factors were seen as better positioned for long-term growth, as they were less exposed to the risks of climate change and better able to adapt to a low-carbon economy. Additionally, governments and regulators around the world have implemented policies to reduce greenhouse gas emissions and encourage the use of renewable energy, creating a business case for companies to improve their environmental performance. This approach reflects the ecosystem lens and looking at all the factors that are impacted and impact the climate as well as at the key decision-makers that can influence the outcomes.

The concept of environmental, social and governance criteria has been around for decades, but in the past couple of years there has been a shift in focus towards better understanding the interlink between people and planet. This shift has been driven by the recognition that sustainability is not just about reducing environmental impact but also about creating social and economic value for all stakeholders.

Yet what has become apparent is that there are three challenges. One is identifying what the 'S' is in the context of organizational change; two, how to measure the change or improvements, and three, where to start in redesigning governance that can meaningfully shift the culture.

Due to these challenges, many organizations are now backsliding into the trend of focusing predominantly on the environment.

Despite the fact that ESG has been put together because there is a link between all three, focus on the 'S' is beginning to dissipate.

One of the most important areas in which the interlink between people and planet can be seen is human rights.

Human rights abuses such as forced labour have a significant negative impact on the environment and on women in particular. Companies that violate human rights are more likely to engage in environmental degradation, deforestation and pollution. Similarly, companies that prioritize environmental sustainability may also be more likely to respect human rights and promote social inclusion.

Another area where the interlink between people and planet is evident is in that of gender equity. Gender equity is not only a moral but also a business imperative. Companies with a gender-diverse leadership and workforce tend to have a higher financial performance and are better able to innovate and adapt to changing market conditions. Gender equity is also linked to environmental sustainability as it helps to ensure that the needs and perspectives of both men and women are taken into account in decision-making processes.

The shift towards understanding the interlink between people and planet has led to a more holistic approach to sustainability. It recognizes that sustainability is not just about reducing environmental impact but also about creating social and economic value for all stakeholders. Companies that prioritize social and governance factors, in addition to environmental factors, are more likely to commit time and resources to learning how their governance and their culture could be negatively affecting Black women. They will understand the need for targeted solutions. They will also ensure that they communicate their strategy to their stakeholders. In understanding the vital role ESG plays in enabling both profits and purpose, they will continue to actively work on both short- and long-term strategies, as they are integral to their growth.

Environmental, social and governance criteria are increasingly being used by investors to evaluate the performance of companies and their potential for long-term growth. Among the social criteria, gender equity is becoming an important consideration for investors as it is linked to a company's overall performance and its ability to create value.

Gender equity refers to flattening the hierarchy among women, by taking an intersectional approach to ensure that there is the same access to opportunities and resources for all women, and is instrumental in achieving gender equality. It includes issues such as equal pay and equal representation in leadership positions. To reiterate, gender equity is not only a moral imperative, but also a business one.

ESG strategies that focus on gender equity will actively seek to increase representation across their pipeline, but also ensure that Black women are included in decision-making processes. For example, companies that have a high proportion of women in leadership roles may be more likely to have policies and practices in place that support gender equity, such as flexible working arrangements and parental leave.

However, it is important to note that simply having a high proportion of women in leadership roles does not guarantee that a company is truly committed to gender equity. Investors must also consider other factors, such as pay equity, representation of women in different levels of the company and whether the company has specific programmes in place to support the advancement of women.

Applying ESG directly to the context of gender equity in the workplace involves considering three main factors: the workplace environment, the social impact and the governance that drives the processes and policies.

The workplace *environment*, the 'E' in ESG, refers to both the physical and cultural aspects of the workplace that can impact gender equity. This includes factors such as the availability of flexible working arrangements, the presence of bias and discrimination and the availability of resources and support for women in the workplace. For example, companies that have a culture of flexible working arrangements and provide resources such as on-site childcare may be more likely to attract and retain women in the workforce.

The *social* impact, the 'S' in ESG, refers to the broader societal impact of a company's policies and practices on gender equity. This includes factors such as pay equity, representation of women in leadership roles and policies that support work–life balance. For example, companies that have a high proportion of women in leadership roles and policies that support work–life balance may be seen as leaders in gender equity and may be more attractive to investors and customers.

The *governance*, the 'G' in ESG, refers to the processes and policies that drive a company's commitment to gender equity. This includes factors such as transparency and accountability, the presence of a diversity and inclusions policy and the availability of training and development opportunities for women. For example, companies that have clear and transparent policies on gender equity, a commitment to diversity and inclusion, and provide training and development opportunities for women may be more likely to achieve gender equity in the workplace.

When applying ESG to the context of gender equity in the workplace, it's important to consider all three factors together. A company may score well on one factor but neglect others, which can lead to an incomplete or ineffective approach to gender equity. Companies that take a holistic approach to ESG and gender equity are more likely to create a workplace environment that is inclusive and equitable for all employees.

Gender equity and sustainability are closely linked, as both are essential for creating a fair and just society. Gender equity refers to the equal distribution of opportunities and resources between men and women, while sustainability is the ability to meet the needs of the present without compromising the ability of future generations to meet their own needs.

One of the key ways in which gender equity and sustainability are linked is through the inclusion of women in decision-making processes. When women are not represented in decision-making roles, their perspectives and needs are often not taken into account, leading to policies and practices that are not inclusive or equitable. This can have a negative impact on sustainability, as it can lead to policies and practices that do not consider the needs of all members of society.

Another link between gender equity and sustainability is through the promotion of work–life balance. When policies and practices do not support this, it can be difficult for women, who are often primary caregivers, to participate in the workforce. This can lead to a gender gap in the workforce, which can in turn have negative impacts on economic growth and sustainability. Policies and practices that support work–life balance, such as flexible working arrangements, parental leave and affordable childcare, can help to promote gender equity and sustainability.

Gender equity is also linked to environmental sustainability. For example, women are often disproportionately affected by climate change and environmental degradation, as they are more likely to rely on natural resources for their livelihoods. Policies and practices that promote gender equity, such as women's participation in decision-making processes and access to resources, can also promote environmental sustainability.

When discussing gender equity or diversity, equity and inclusion, there is a tendency to focus on one element, either the 'E' or the 'S', Yet, focusing on only one element of ESG can have negative consequences for both the company and its stakeholders.

For example, a company that only focuses on environmental factors may neglect important social and governance considerations. This can lead to a lack of attention to issues such as labour rights, human rights and gender equity, which can result in reputational damage and financial penalties. Additionally, a company that only focuses on environmental factors may miss out on the benefits of addressing social and governance considerations, such as engaged employees, satisfied customers and supportive communities.

Similarly, a company that only focuses on social factors may neglect important environmental and governance considerations. This can lead to a lack of attention to issues such as carbon emissions, energy efficiency and renewable energy, which can result in reputational damage and financial penalties. Additionally, a company that only focuses on social factors may miss out on the benefits of addressing environmental and governance considerations, such as a reduced risk of climate change and improved risk management.

A company that only focuses on governance factors may also neglect important environmental and social considerations. This can lead to a lack of attention to issues such as carbon emissions, labour rights and human rights, which can result in reputational damage and financial penalties. Additionally, a company that only focuses on governance factors may miss out on the benefits of addressing environmental and social considerations, such as a reduced risk of climate change and engaged employees.

In conclusion, it is important for companies to consider all three elements of ESG when evaluating their performance and potential for long-term growth. A holistic approach to ESG can help companies to identify and manage risks, create opportunities for growth and ultimately create a more sustainable and responsible business.

The role of stakeholders in promoting progress towards gender equity and ESG initiatives is critical. Stakeholders include investors, customers, employees and the broader community, and they can all play a role in promoting progress in these areas.

Investors, for example, can use their influence and financial power to push companies to prioritize gender equity and ESG initiatives. They can do this by engaging with companies, voting on proposals related to these issues and supporting companies that have strong track records on gender equity and ESG. They can also use their influence to push for changes in regulations and policies that support these initiatives.

Customers can also play a role in promoting progress by choosing to do business with companies that prioritize gender equity and ESG. They can also use their voice to advocate for these issues, for example by signing petitions or joining campaigns that call on companies to improve their performance on gender equity and ESG.

Employees can also play a key role in promoting progress by advocating for gender equity and ESG initiatives within their own companies. They can do this by speaking up about issues, participating in employee resource groups and supporting company-wide initiatives that promote these issues.

The broader community also plays a role in promoting progress by raising awareness about the importance of gender equity and ESG and pushing for changes in policies and regulations that support these initiatives. This can be done through community activism, grassroots campaigns and pressuring government officials to take action.

Much like ESG scoring, a granular and specific analysis is necessary to drive change, particularly when it comes to gender equity. A sustainable approach to governance is one that is embedded in the operations of an organization, regardless of the presence of an advocate or champion. Without a focus on social factors, such as diversity, equity and inclusion, organizations risk missing out on the benefits of a more inclusive and equitable workplace, which can lead to poor financial outcomes.

Focusing solely on environmental and governance factors, without considering the social aspect of the workplace, is inadequate for achieving sustainable business practice. A comprehensive approach to ESG is necessary, one that takes into account the interlink between the environment, society and governance. This includes not only the physical environment, but also the cultural and social environment of the workplace, including diversity, equity and inclusion.

As organizations recognize the increasing pressure to develop the necessary knowledge, experience and resources, as well as governance structures, to effectively address and manage climate-related risks and other material ESG issues, such as human rights violations within their supply chains, it is crucial for directors and senior management to possess a strong level of expertise and understanding in these areas. However, it is also vital to recognize the importance of diverse perspectives and experiences among all members of the board and management team.

This is where diversity can make a crucial difference. A diverse group of individuals brings a range of unique perspectives and skills that can greatly enhance a company's ability to effectively navigate and comply with the ever-evolving ESG expectations set by regulators. The different perspectives and varied knowledge, experience and resources of a diverse board, particularly one that includes under-represented groups such as Black women, can help meet the myriad ESG-related expectations that regulators continue to develop for corporate management. This is particularly important as Black women are often overlooked as a demographic in ESG and sustainability discussions, despite the fact that they are disproportionately affected by environmental and social issues.

A sustainable governance approach is one that is embedded in the operations of the organization, and that serves the organization without the presence of an advocate or champion.

CHAPTER TEN

How to Create a Values-based Environment

Changing the governance changes the cultural. When I refer to organizational governance I am referring to the systems, processes and structures that are in place to guide decision-making, manage risk and ensure accountability within an organization – the three key facets of organizational governance.

The board of directors are responsible for setting the strategic direction of the organization, overseeing management and ensuring that the organization is operating in a legal and ethical manner. They are a key part of holding organizations accountable and critical in ensuring that diversity, equity and inclusion targets are implemented. Not only that, they also need to believe in the importance of supporting and accelerating gender equity. Without their buy-in, it will be impossible to implement any strategies. Profit does not have to be sacrificed for purpose and a board of directors with this view will be fundamental to organizations that will have long-term success.

Policies and procedures are created as best practices. Organizations should have clear policies and procedures in place to guide decision-making, manage risk and ensure compliance with laws and regulations. The difficulty for most organizations is being able to critically analyze who these policies and procedures benefit and disadvantage. This is what sets apart a values-based organization. They understand that values are also driven by policies and procedure.

Then the final piece of governance is internal controls, the systems and processes that are put in place to ensure that the organization is operating efficiently, effectively and in accordance with its policies and procedures. Examples of internal controls include financial controls, risk management processes and information security measures. Internal controls uphold the values expressed in the policies and procedures.

In creating a values-based environment, accountability is actively embedded in both policies and procedures that have an impact externally, but also on the internal controls, and part of that is people management. The dynamic nature of a values-based environment also means that there is an open approach to continuously checking and measuring to what extent their values are being lived.

As the values of organizations are being more closely questioned it has become clearer that there is an increasing divergence between the externally promoted values and how they are implemented internally.

The 3 Cs of a healthy culture are clarity, consistency and cohesion. All three of these need to be implemented simultaneously, otherwise organizations quickly move into performative territory.

Clarity in messaging is essential. For example, it is not enough for an organization to say that they stand with certain groups without providing tangible details. How do they plan to support these groups and what is the hoped-for impact? The other important factor is the emphasis on why this topic is important. A lack of clarity is one of the principle reasons why diversity, equity and inclusion initiatives often lack the necessary support.

DEI may be called a business imperative, but, without providing clarity as to why, it can appear that the organization is simply following a trend and not taking it seriously.

There is still a lack of trust between leadership and their employee base, as it pertains to how genuine the organization's commitment is to gender equity, and this is because of a lack of cohesion. There is a clear line between what is done externally and internally. For example, signing a charter that supports increased female representation in leadership, but not wanting to address the gender equity issues internally and still actively avoiding conversations around the support and promotion of Black women in their organization.

The final pillar is consistency of effort. Many organizations try to show support by taking part in celebrations and focusing on the diversity calendar, for example Black History Month and International Women's History Month, yet during the rest of year little is actually done to support the groups.

Critically analyzing the 3C principles is to ask, honestly, if your organization is delivering on all three or if your focus is on one element only. Without activating all three elements in tandem the chances are that your employees are not aware of your values and certainly will not be convinced that they are being lived.

Values are the guiding principles that shape the culture and behaviour of an organization. They are the foundation upon which a company is built and they should influence every decision made and every action taken within the organization. A values-based organization is one that is committed to upholding its core values in all aspects of its business.

Organizations that prioritize creating a values-based environment view it as critical to organizational success and how it relates to the wellbeing, satisfaction and productivity of its employees.

This includes creating a culture where employees feel valued and respected, fostering open and honest communication, providing opportunities for professional development and growth and promoting inclusivity and diversity.

It would be both idealistic and unrealistic to ignore the discomfort that comes with implementing such change and the resistance that organizations may face; but exploring the common challenges that you may encounter when trying to implement a values-based environment – such as lack of buy-in from leadership, lack of clear communication and the importance of the leadership as role models for the values that they are trying to instil in the organization – aids the journey.

Research has shown that organizations that create a values-based environment have lower employee turnover, increased employee engagement and improved productivity and creativity. Ultimately, organizations that focus on creating a values-based environment are better positioned not only to attract but also to retain top talent and also to become more resilient in the face of future challenges.

Values cannot and do not exist in a bubble separate from societal and economic challenges and this is why organizational resilience must also be interlaced with a values-based strategy.

Organizational resilience refers to an organization's ability to anticipate, prepare for and adapt to unexpected events and changes in a way that allows it to maintain or quickly resume critical operations and functions. In the context of promoting gender equity, organizational resilience is important because it allows an organization to respond effectively and efficiently to the unique challenges and obstacles that Black women and other marginalized groups may face in the workplace.

Proactivity and analysis underpin an organization's ability to be resilient. Taking a macro- and micro-view of the economy, global growth, trends in social awareness and justice and people and planet means that organizations are better able to anticipate and prepare for the types of challenges and obstacles that Black women may encounter in the workplace. This could include identifying and addressing sexist and racist practices in the hiring and promotion processes, as well as creating more inclusive and equitable policies and procedure to counteract them.

Bureaucracy is the enemy of progress and causes many organizations to lose marginalized and minoritized employees because they are unwilling to be adaptable and responsive in the face of change. Without this level of flexibility, they are ill-equipped to change course quickly and efficiently when faced with unexpected challenges or obstacles, and the ability to pivot and make adjustments to policies, processes and programmes as needed. This can be seen in the resistance to closing gender pay gaps within organizations, which is usually caused by a belief that is requires both too much bureaucracy and the sacrifice of profit for purpose.

As we move into a more turbulent economic phase, leaders are being driven to find ways to generate profits, which is usually done through job cuts. Resilient organizations are not sheltered from this, but they are better able to manage critical operations and functions. They still monitor the impact on minoritized and marginalized groups and actively continue to support and advance their careers. During the pandemic, Black employees, women and other minoritized groups were hit the hardest by job cuts. Resilient and values-based organizations take a more holistic and considered approach to letting people go even in the face of financial challenges.

In line with the 3C principles, resilience promotes a culture of learning and continuous improvement; it is crucial for organizations to identify and fix their own issues, and not just solve them but prevent them in the future and create the space to address issues related to equity and representation of marginalized groups, access to opportunity and impact on the community.

By building organizational resilience, an organization will be better positioned to create an equitable workplace for Black women and will continue to position and reposition itself to respond effectively to unexpected events or changes that may impact its ability to promote gender equity.

Another key aspect of a values-based organization is accountability. When all employees are held accountable for their actions and behaviours, it helps to create a culture of integrity and trust. It also ensures that the organization is operating both efficiently and effectively, as everyone is working towards shared goals and objectives.

Here are some steps your organization can take to create a values-based environment with a focus on accountability:

- Identify and define your core values: the first step in creating a values-based organization is to identify and define your core values. These are the principles that guide the behaviour of your organization and shape its culture. It is important to choose values that are meaningful to your organization and align with your mission and vision.
- Communicate your values: once you have identified your core values, it is important to communicate them to all members of your organization.

This can be done through team meetings, company-wide emails, and by including them in your employee handbook and other company documents. It is important that everyone understands what the values are and what they mean.

- Model your values: it is important for leaders and managers to model the behaviour that aligns with your values. This helps to create a culture in which values are not just words on a page, but are actively demonstrated and upheld. If employees see their leaders living the values, they are more likely to do so as well.

- Embed your values in all aspects of your business: your values should influence every decision made and action taken within your organization. This includes things like hiring, performance evaluations and project prioritization. For example, if one of your values is integrity, you might prioritize hiring candidates who demonstrate high levels of integrity in their work and personal lives.

- Regularly review and reaffirm your values: it is important to regularly review and reaffirm your values to ensure that they remain relevant and aligned with the needs of your organization. This can be done through team meetings and surveys to gather feedback from employees.

- Clearly define roles and responsibilities: to hold people accountable, it is important to make sure that each employee understands their role and what is expected of them. This can be done through job descriptions, training and regular check-ins.

- Set clear goals and expectations: set specific, measurable, achievable, relevant and time-bound (SMART) goals for each employee and make sure they understand what is expected of them. This will help them to focus their efforts and know what success looks like.

- Monitor progress and provide feedback: regularly check in with employees to see how they are progressing towards their goals and provide constructive feedback to help them stay on track. This can be done through one-on-one meetings, team meetings and regular performance evaluations.

- Hold people accountable: if someone is not meeting their goals or responsibilities, it is important to have a conversation about it and work together to find a solution. This might involve additional training, setting more specific goals or providing additional support.
- Offer support and resources: provide employees with the support and resources they need to be successful in their roles. This may include training, tools and guidance. By investing in your employees, you are showing true commitment to your values and to their progression.

Rehumanizing employees also sits at the heart of being values-driven. Employee satisfaction is not ignored, but prioritized. Unfortunately, many leaders forget that the employer/employee relationship is a mutually beneficial one. They do not believe in providing extra benefits, because the underlying belief is that each employee should feel grateful to have a job.

While this may not be stated, it will be reflected in holiday pay, working flexibility, maternity leave terms and conditions, pension contributions and healthcare contributions.

In a truly equitable organization, benefits and support systems are not seen as perks, but as necessities. This includes things like parental leave, flexible working arrangements and mental health support. These benefits and support systems are not just nice-to-haves, but are fundamental to the wellbeing and productivity of employees. By providing these benefits and support systems, organizations are investing in your employees and showing that they value and care for their wellbeing. This, in turn, leads to increased employee satisfaction, engagement and loyalty, all of which benefit the organization in the long run.

Employees are an investment, not a cost. Organizations are not charities and they should generate profit, but not at the expense or the wellbeing of their employees. There are many ways to invest in employees and it does not always have to be with a pay rise. It can also be in the form of the aforementioned benefits.

The ability of an organization to succeed in accelerating gender equity is by embedding it within its values, to push forward with this lens applied to every part of the process and ultimately being open and willing to learn. At every point in this process, feedback will be required and the defining factor is what will be done with this feedback.

Putting feedback into action builds trust in the willingness and commitment of an organization. Collecting feedback also creates community in generating an opportunity to bring together people of different seniority levels, backgrounds, races and ethnicities, so that they can contribute to crafting the values. This then ensures that the values reflect the ethos of the business and its staff.

Authenticity in values increases the chances of success, as irrelevant or unrealistic values are impossible to live by. An inclusive approach to value creation that actively engages marginalized and minority groups leads to more equitable outcomes. Ensuring that all voices are heard and represented within the decision-making process increases the likelihood that individuals' goals and beliefs are taken into consideration.

CHAPTER ELEVEN

Employers of the Future

As the world continues to grapple with the impact of the COVID-19 pandemic and the ongoing issues of racial injustice, the need for resilient organizations has become more pressing than ever. Businesses must be able to anticipate and react to change in order to remain competitive and meet the evolving needs of their employees and clients.

The murder of George Floyd and the subsequent protests have brought issues of racial injustice and equity to the forefront of society's consciousness. This has led to a greater awareness of the ways in which these issues are present in the workplace and the need for organizations to take action to address them.

As a result, the employer/employee relationship has shifted, with a greater emphasis being placed on mutual benefit and the need for organizations to take a more active role in promoting equity and inclusivity. This shift has led to a change in the power dynamic between employers and employees, with employees now expecting organizations to do more in order to attract and retain talent.

As economies continue to struggle in the wake of the pandemic, the relationship between employers and employees has become increasingly complex. Employers are facing financial pressures and must make difficult decisions to stay afloat, while employees are grappling with their own financial concerns and the uncertainty of the future.

In this context, organizations that are able to anticipate and react to change, while also recognizing the importance of the employer/employee relationship, are more likely to be successful in attracting and retaining high-potential talent.

There are several approach changes that, as employers, organizations will need to consider, which can also support their gender equity efforts.

Internal mobility

At the end of 2022 and beginning of 2023, many companies started to announce hiring freezes, which not only meant that they had to rethink their gender equality strategy with hiring being the focus, but that they could now turn to retention as the focus to accelerate their gender equity efforts.

Internal mobility strategies can be an effective way to address evolving needs and priorities without changes in headcount. By focusing on internal talent mobility, they can help existing employees develop new skills and take on new responsibilities, which can help to meet evolving organizational needs.

Offering stretch and upskilling opportunities can also help to develop the capabilities of existing employees and ensure that they are equipped to handle new challenges. Leveraging alumni networks and gig workers can provide organizations with a flexible way to bring in talent on an as-needed basis.

Focusing on internal talent also requires all managers to become more familiar with the talent pool within the organization. A reassessment of who is a high-potential candidate will also present opportunities for those who may have been overlooked for a promotion, but with this new approach they may be able to expand their role.

These strategies can help organizations to be more agile and responsive to changing needs, while also supporting the growth and development of their employees.

How can this internal mobility be a career changer for Black women?

Historically, internal mobility within organizations has often been informal and based on personal connections, which has tended to benefit White men the most. This is because they were more likely to have established networks and relationships within the organization, which they could leverage to advance their careers. This informal system of internal mobility has perpetuated the existing power dynamics and privileges within the organization, which disproportionately benefits White men.

This has led to a lack of diversity in leadership positions, as women and people of colour have been under-represented in these roles. This also has an impact on the culture of the organization as the lack of diversity in leadership means that the organization may not be able to understand the diverse needs and perspective of its employees and customers.

Internal mobility is a powerful tool that organizations can use to create non-traditional career pathways, promote diversity and inclusivity, and build a more resilient workforce. By providing employees with opportunities to advance within the organization, based on their ability to perform, knowledge of the company and potential, rather than on their personal connections, organizations can create a more level playing field for all employees.

When internal mobility is used in this way, it can help to break down the traditional power dynamics that have previously existed within organizations, and create opportunities for under-represented groups, such as women and people of colour, to advance in their careers.

Internal mobility, despite its informal nature, still requires a supporting process and job or responsibility specification sheet to be effective. This is particularly important for Black women, who often face barriers to success, such as lack of access to information and networks. Without a clear and transparent process in place, Black women may not have access to the information they need in order to apply for and secure internal mobility opportunities.

A supporting process and job or responsibility specification sheet can help to ensure that all employees, regardless of their background or network connections, have access to the same information and are able to apply for internal mobility opportunities. This can include clear guidelines for the application process, as well as detailed job descriptions and an outline of the qualifications required for the role.

Democratizing access to information is crucial to internal mobility, as it is to the promotion process. This means having clear lines of communication, ensuring that all decision-makers, managers and eligible employees are informed at the same time, and providing a timeline for the process. By providing equal access to information and a transparent process, organizations can ensure that all employees have the opportunity to apply for internal mobility opportunities and advance in their careers based on merit.

It's also important to note that internal mobility should not be seen as an opportunity to allocate more work without extra remuneration; there should be clear guidelines and compensation for any additional responsibilities and workload.

Internal mobility can also be an opportunity for organizations to address long-standing issues of institutional bias and to actively seek out and promote under-represented groups such as Black women. By focusing on equity and creating opportunities for these groups, organizations can create a more diverse and inclusive workforce, which can lead to increased innovation, productivity and overall success.

Hybrid flexibility

Hybrid working and flexibility around how and where we work is here to stay for the most part. The fight by employers to get their staff back into the office full time has been an uphill battle and in general it seems that employees have won.

It should not seem so strange to accept a work arrangement that allows employees to combine remote working with in-office working, as it was mandated by governments, but there are still doubts about its success.

For Black women, however, working for home has given them the space to try to recover from the constant onslaught of microaggressions through to outright racism. Applying a gender equity lens means understanding that until more of the system is fixed, more Black women will want to have this hybrid work pattern, or even to choose to work from home completely.

The upsides of this type of flexibility are clear. It can provide employees with the ability to choose where and when they work and can help to increase productivity and engagement.

Hybrid flexibility has positive effects for both the individual and for the organization and can serve the needs of both.

Hybrid flexibility can allow employees to work from a location that is most conducive to their productivity, whether that is at home, in a co-working space or in the office. It acknowledges each individual's needs and allows them maximize time spent in the environment best suited to them.

Flexibility is part of the values-based environment that rehumanizes employees by supporting them in achieving a better work–life balance. The ability to be able to balance work and personal commitments without fear of asking for time for appointments, or being made to feel guilty if a child is often sick, is priceless for many employees. This deepens the employees' loyalty to the organization, which in turn makes it easier to attract and retain talent.

The Experience Chasm Survey 2021 shows that 25 per cent of Black women decide to join an organization based on the experiences of other Black women. When hybrid working is one of the defence mechanisms for Black women in the workplace, this will be an important factor in those discussions.

However, there is a downside to hybrid working that has given rise to a new kind of ceiling – the 'Zoom Ceiling', which is defined as being overlooked for promotion due to working from home and therefore having less visibility in the office itself. As women and minoritized groups tend to prefer to work from home, it can exacerbate the situation for Black women in particular.

How can the Zoom Ceiling be tackled?

The presence culture is still rewarded, which can lead those who work remotely to feel not only an increased sense of isolation, but also worried about their diminishing career opportunities. Establishing specific dates for critical strategic meetings, whether virtual or in person, will help to work against this.

Coffee-machine conversations cannot be prevented and may be where ideas are bounced around, but here is where transparency and communication can change the dynamic. If ideas discussed are shared online, it gives those who work remotely the confidence that they are also in the loop and that their contribution has the same weight and importance as those who are in the office.

Organized gatherings are not restricted to work only; they can be an opportunity to spend time with colleagues socially to foster open communication and a team feeling.

By reviewing and adjusting promotion criteria, organizations can be prompted to look closely at the criteria for determining whether they are skewed towards face-to-face interactions or in-office presence. Seeking alignment with remote working will also help to ensure that remote workers are not disadvantaged. The challenge that remote working presents is that it can make it harder for managers to evaluate their employees' performance as they miss out on some of the non-verbal cues.

Therefore, training should be provided to managers on how to evaluate employees remotely by focusing on objective criteria, such as quality of work, meeting deadlines and the ability to work remotely. Regular check-ins and progress reports can be helpful in evaluating employee performance remotely.

Hybrid working is going to be one of the tougher situations to navigate, so what should the priority be? For Black women, it is that they have the psychological and physical safety they need.

Without this, they will not be able to do their jobs to the best of their ability.

Therefore, having flexibility is so important for the Black woman as well as ensuring that there are no processes that inadvertently undermine your organization's commitment to it. Has your organization been clear on its standpoint on hybrid working or is it at the discretion of each manager?

What are the criteria of a job that must be done from the office? The benchmark for this is: was this job done from home during the pandemic or from the office?

If hybrid working is not a standard option for everyone, is there a cumbersome approval process for requesting flexible or hybrid working?

A provision is not equal to being able to do something. Companies may say that they offer flexible working policies in order to make themselves attractive to new employees, but in practice managers may not actually approve flexible or hybrid working when employees ask for it.

Manager upskilling

Providing fresh support and training to managers can help to alleviate the pressure that they may be feeling and also to mitigate the widening managerial skills gap. As the needs and expectations of employees continue to evolve, it is important for managers to have access to the latest tools and techniques to help them effectively lead and support their teams.

Clarifying manager priorities and making it clear how managers should allocate their time can also help to relieve pressure on them. By redesigning roles where necessary and providing clear guidance on what is expected of managers, organizations can help to ensure that they are able to focus on the tasks and responsibilities that are most important for achieving business goals.

By taking these two key actions, organizations can help to support the development of their managers and create a more effective and efficient workforce.

Black women have long spoken out about their managers needing to learn about racial equity and intersectionality as part of their roles. Lack of inclusive management is a skills gap that should be addressed at each level within an organization, to help to develop the skill of seeing Black women as human beings, not as functions.

The focus on inclusive leadership has meant that this information is reserved for the upper echelons of a business, but by rolling out this training at all managerial levels and adding it to performance objectives, inclusive leadership will be measured by 360-degree feedback. This not only promotes a healthy information flow, but also embeds accountability in the organization through management.

Change in hiring practice

In order to fill critical roles in the near future, it will be important to assess candidates based on their ability to perform in the role, rather than just on their credentials and previous experience. This may require organizations to rethink their traditional assumptions about qualifications and consider a broader range of candidates who may have the skills and abilities needed to succeed in the role.

Hiring criteria are based on credentials on paper rather than the ability to perform. By considering candidates based on the latter, organizations may be able to increase the diversity of their workforce and create a more inclusive culture.

With the focus being on talent and their ability to perform, rather than stereotypical credentials, organizations may be able to improve the overall performance of their workforce while at the same time challenging assumptions of what capable staff look like and what degrees and certificates they need to have.

Hiring bias is such that the more we see one demographic in a role, the more we believe that this is the only demographic that can successfully do the job. By being open and flexible in considering a broader range of candidates, organizations may be able to find individuals who have the skills and experience required to meet the changing needs of the business.

Overall, it will be important for organizations to be open to new ways of assessing candidates and to consider a range of factors beyond traditional qualifications in order to fill critical roles in the years to come.

We have slowly come to realize that not everyone learns the same way, that not everyone needs to go to university, and this is going to drive a change in the landscape of the workplace.

Looking it at from the fix-the-system standpoint, you need to determine what the necessary hurdle was to gain access. By readjusting or, rather, removing some arbitrary standards, can you open the doors to a lot more capable and talented people?

Pandemic PTSD

The pandemic has had a significant impact on the mental health and wellbeing of many individuals, so addressing and supporting employees through pandemic-related trauma will be part of the responsibility of employers of the future.

The impact of the pandemic has forever changed several generations. The breadth and depth of the damage is still unknown and has not been spoken about enough within the workplace as the rush has been to return to normality and try to forget the pandemic. From a societal standpoint, we have spoken about increased rates of loneliness and depression and feelings of isolation, but we have not spoken about the anxiety many are battling with when faced with the return to the office and coming back into contact with people. For some, having a video call was the only contact they had with another person in a day or sometimes in a week.

Even within organizations that do not offer hybrid working, having a staggered entry back into the office may need to be a part of a plan for some and there needs to be room to have these discussions.

The role of the employer is also to help support employees with their anxiety and accept that not all, but some, will be feeling the effects of being locked down for a long time. Anxiety and discomfort will influence how employees perform.

Pandemic PTSD is a relatively new concept, but talking about it within the workplace will normalize the topic and encourage those who are suffering to seek help. Organizations can help with this by hiring an external expert to introduce the topic into the workplace and providing tips on recognition of symptoms and information on resources and support; by working together with an expert to provide employees with access to mental health resources and support, such as counselling services; and by creating employee assistance programmes and providing anonymous hotline access.

The support that an employer can also provide is socializing the topic with the help of an expert with Human Resources and managers, so that they can also enhance their skills in learning how to recognize, support and ensure there is care for any employees who may be suffering from PTSD. This might include the introduction of a return-to-the-office policy that allows for a staggered return over the course of six months, for example.

The stigma of talking about mental health issues for Black women, thanks to the stereotype of the 'strong Black woman', might mean that she will not talk about the issues she is facing to her managers or colleagues. Having a return-to-office policy along with an anonymous hotline resource will allow her to feel more comfortable and supported without the threat of having her position or the perception of her compromised.

DEI pushback

With increasing reports that diversity, equity and inclusion initiatives have not delivered the promised results, many leaders are questioning the relevance and benefits of dedicating resources to it.

The promised innovation and improvements to the bottom line have failed to materialize, and there is emerging fatigue in discussing the topic.

We have got to this stage for three reasons:

1) a knee-jerk reaction drove an influx of practitioners yet fewer experts;
2) quick-fix solutions, tips and hacks were provided, mostly in the form of workshops;

3) a one-size-fits-all methodology was advocated: if it works for one marginalized or minoritized group, then it will work for all other minoritized and marginalized groups.

The result of all three has left a lot of organizations in a seemingly worse position than when they started on their journey and, if this is where your organization is, then I want to confirm to you that you are also standing at the beginning of an opportunity to reshape and redirect your organization's journey.

Diversity is the goal that organizations should aim for, with equity and inclusion being the tools used to achieve this. Under the umbrella of diversity are nine protected characteristics. Equity is different for each group, especially when you have intersecting identities, such as Black women.

With that in mind, specificity is the only true driver of meaningful change, but the approach cannot be from an educational perspective. Workshops are most powerful immediately after participation, but without practical application and consistent information flow, they fail to create the necessary feeling of importance and impact.

Taking an ecosystem lens approach involves bringing cohesion and consistency to your own approach, through trying to tackle one problem within the many parts of the business that influence the issue.

Let's say an employee complains about a lack of clarity and communication around the company's promotion and advancement process. The HR department decides to take an ecosystem lens approach to address this complaint. They identify all the different parts of the business that could contribute to the problem, such as the company's promotion and advancement policies, the employee's awareness and understanding of these policies and the communications channels used to convey these policies to employees.

Once the HR department has identified all the different parts of the business that could be contributing to the problem, they can then take a cohesive and consistent approach to addressing it. For example, they might review and revamp the company's promotion and advancement policies, make sure that employees are aware of these policies and have access to training on them, and explore new ways to communicate these policies more effectively, such as through company-wide meetings, training sessions and regular updates via internal intranet or portal.

By taking this ecosystem lens approach, the HR department is able to address the employee's complaint in a comprehensive and holistic way, rather than simply focusing on one specific aspect of the business, and ensure that the entire system is aligned to promote fairness and transparency in the promotion process.

Just like using an ecosystem lens, achieving equity takes time and investment and there are no shortcuts.

Looking at all the moving parts is no small endeavour, so promises of quick solutions have historically been falsely made and have done DEI work a considerable disservice. Implementing such deep and large-scale changes in an organization, irrespective of its size, will not happen overnight and many of the governance changes being made now will only bear fruit in three years' time.

Viewing DEI work as an investment and bearing in mind that a typical investment cycle is usually three to five years, it is unrealistic to promise significant organizational transformation in a short period of time. When embarking on a transformation journey, it's important to manage the expectations of leadership and minority or marginalized groups within the organization to prevent disappointment and maintain long-term engagement and support for the initiative.

DEI work is not a one-time initiative, it's an ongoing process. Even after an initial investment period, the work must be continuously monitored, evaluated and adapted as needed to ensure progress is sustained and the organization remains in alignment and on target.

This is worth the effort, since, the benefits of DEI initiatives go beyond just making the workplace more inclusive for minority or marginalized groups; they also benefit the entire organization by creating a more engaged, productive and innovative workforce. They also help attract and retain top talent, and can improve the organization's reputation, which can lead to increased business opportunities and revenue.

DEI work must also be led from the top, and all employees must be held accountable for upholding the values and principles of the organization. Without a strong commitment from leadership and a culture of accountability, DEI initiatives are likely to falter.

Another side of the current pushback also underscores why it is important for organizations to do their due diligence on the expertise of their providers. It is important for organizations to work with experts who have a deep understanding of the issues related to diversity, equity and inclusion, and who can provide guidance on how to effectively implement these principles in the workplace. These experts should have a broad understanding of the current employment trends, economic shifts and relevant regulations and corporate social responsibility requirements. By working with experts who understand the broader context of DEI issues, organizations can ensure that their DEI initiatives are integrated into their overall business strategy and that they are able to achieve meaningful, sustainable change.

The other consequence of this pushback is that organizations are quietly reducing their efforts, which further excludes marginalized and minoritized groups, because they are struggling to demonstrate the success of their initiatives so far.

There may be a variety of factors that contribute to the pushback, such as resistance to change or misunderstanding of the purpose of DEI initiatives; these should be addressed, but should not be allowed to derail plans for creating an equitable workplace for all.

As we continue to move further forward into the phase of measurement and accountability, there will be an increasing drive to demonstrate results and this is why being prepared and anticipating this will be vital in facing internal headwinds. Building a strategy that has specificity at its core will facilitate the changes that many sceptics have yet to see.

Progress may be slow, but moving in the right direction is the most important thing. In the face of pushback, it is key to be able to highlight progress while reinforcing the understanding that time and effort are required to address the underlying issues and structural barriers that have led to the underrepresentation and marginalization of Black women in the workplace. Indeed, these are the one ways in which true and lasting change can be achievable.

How to lean into the discomfort of change

Accelerating gender equity in an organization is not easy and requires a willingness to acknowledge and address the systemic barriers that have led to the underrepresentation and marginalization of Black women. It requires a commitment to challenging the status quo.

One of the key challenges in addressing these issues is the discomfort that it can create. When addressing issues of equity and inclusion, it is important to recognize that these are complex and multifaceted problems that can be difficult to navigate. It can be uncomfortable to confront one's own biases and privilege, and to confront the ways in which systemic barriers have perpetuated inequality. However, it is important to remember that discomfort is a sign that change is happening and that progress is being made.

Whether on an individual or organizational level, the fear of getting it wrong can prevent commitment and action. These fears are not unfounded, as there is no space in the court of public opinion to get things wrong, but one of the ways to negate this is by being vulnerable. Change is uncomfortable, but it is important to acknowledge and embrace this discomfort. The default can be to talk about aspirational goals and not admit that they are aspirational. However, part of the process of leaning into the discomfort of change is the ability of leaders to be open and honest about the challenges the organization is facing and the fact that they are on a learning curve that will require navigation and some course correction. This honesty and frankness can encourage others in leadership to follow suit. It also removes the pressure of always needing to be right, while maintaining the focus on achieving gender equity through collaboration.

When working to accelerate gender equity, it is important for leaders to recognize that their own perspective and experiences may not always align with the needs and perspectives of Black women. This is why it is crucial to prioritize employee input and actively seek out the perspectives and ideas of Black women.

Actively seeking out employee input can be done in a variety of ways, such as through focus groups, surveys or one-on-one interviews. It is important to create a safe and inclusive space where Black women can share their experiences and ideas, and to ensure that their input is valued and taken into consideration when making decisions.

It is also important not to put Black women in a vulnerable position; this might mean creating a safe space where they can share their ideas and perspectives without fear of retaliation or negative consequences. This might mean that what the situation requires could be a moderated conversation with or without the presence of leaders.

There is often a difference between what leaders think are good ideas versus what actually works, and there has to be the space to actively listen, even if it may feel as if what they are hearing contradicts their worldview.

In centring the needs of Black women, the way they feel most comfortable sharing their perspectives and experiences has to take precedence over leaders' needs to be involved in every part of the process. It is uncomfortable knowing that Black women may not want to share their opinions in front of certain leaders, but that should in no way derail the process.

For most senior leaders, their role in accelerating gender equity is twofold. They are decision-makers, but they should also accept their role as allies. Their focus is not only to amplify the voice of Black women within their organization, but also to actively dismantle the institutional barriers.

In their function as allies, they will constantly be confronted with a different worldview, which may be difficult and uncomfortable to hear.

However, leaders should in fact seek to find the issues around which perspectives may differ because while it may be uncomfortable learning about these perspectives, they are crucial to the experience of becoming and being an ally.

Part of embracing vulnerability and having an open mindset means accepting the truth of these experiences.

There is no perfect way of leaning into the discomfort of change – it is a journey that will require adaptability and the ability to pivot, but there are two principles to bear in mind:

1) Transparency is crucial when it comes to change. By keeping the lines of communication open and communicating honestly about the progress that is being made and the challenges that still need to be overcome, organizations emphasize the importance of all the stakeholders, while also building trust and creating a sense of shared purpose.

2) Holding accountability. Leaning into the discomfort of change means honestly and continuously assessing the progress and adjusting the strategy accordingly. This means leaders regularly measuring the effectiveness of their efforts, identifying what is and isn't working and making adjustments as needed.

CHAPTER TWELVE

Why the Advancement of Black Women Benefits Everyone

The advancement of Black women in the workplace benefits everyone else, but the question is how?

As you go on your gender equity journey, you will no doubt face this question from many sources, and being able to answer it confidently will help in being able to assuage concerns and worries that other groups are being disadvantaged in the process. This section should serve as a support system for addressing these challenges. While there should not need to be a reason to justify gender equity work, not everyone has started their own personal journey and it is important to meet each person where they are and not where we would like them to be.

The power structure is the best starting point. The problem of institutional barriers to gender equity is rooted in power structures, where certain groups are disproportionately represented and hold more power in society, hence their experiences and perspectives become the norm, and others are marginalized. In focusing on gender equity, you will be highlighting how these power structures work and that the impact of them is not present just in the workplace, but also in society and education.

Advancing Black women in the workplace challenges the narrative that exists around their capabilities and values and it brings others on their own journey in having to challenge their own assumptions. In many instances, the burden falls directly on Black women to do the heavy lifting of educating their colleagues to ensure that their immediate environment is easier to work in. They still have to work to validate their presence as being justified and ultimately prove that they are not an intruder. With organizational support, the implication will no longer be that they are intruders, but that they belong in the workplace just as much as any other group and with same amount of access to opportunity, networks and career progression.

As it becomes normalized that a Black woman belongs in decision-making rooms and in leadership positions, the less it will need to be celebrated that she is the first or the only one. There will be no need to focus on her being the standard of Black excellence, but, rather, that Black excellence is a standard.

It is impossible to consider gender equity in isolation, because it is acknowledged that there are not two separate versions of self: the professional and the private. This is why advancing Black women will also have a broader positive impact. When your organization works to dismantle institutional barriers, it will also help dismantle them for others. In learning about the nuanced challenges Black women face, an organization's ability to democratize and streamline processes will automatically include a wider, not narrower, group of people. This means that even if the changes were made because of Black women, other women, for example, will also benefit.

When working with those who face the greatest challenge, you will be widening your scope rather than narrowing it. Gender equality has in many ways allowed organizations to become myopic in their approach, which has led to White women making strides in progress while Black women have been left behind.

In focusing on gender equity, namely flattening the hierarchy among women, any organization can accelerate gender equality efforts. Gender equity works hand-in-hand with gender equality and can lead to a more inclusive and equitable work environment.

The existing hierarchical structure among women, still very evident in the workplace, serves to perpetuate power imbalances and to make it more difficult for Black women to access leadership positions and decision-making power. This is seen when organizations celebrate achieving their targets of 30 per cent female representation in leadership, but on closer analysis there are neither Black women nor women of colour on the team. When this hierarchy is flattened, it creates the same access to opportunities for all women to take on leadership roles, and to have their voices heard and contributions recognized at all levels of the organization. This helps to break down barriers to Black women's advancement and promote greater representation in leadership positions.

Flattening the hierarchy will help your organization to embed long-term change, as representation will have a new meaning. By establishing equitable foundations, Black women's participation in decision-making will be fully integrated, thus heightening their sense of belonging, which has a direct impact on corporate culture and productivity. The other benefit of valuing other perspectives is that it can help to ensure that equitable solutions remain a part of your organization's management style, with the added benefit of challenging the stereotypes and viewpoints that have formed part of institutional barriers.

Moreover, having more diverse representation in leadership positions will inspire more women to pursue leadership roles, and provide role models for other women to follow. This can accelerate the progress by giving more women the opportunity to take on leadership roles and make decisions that affect the direction and success of the organization.

This book emphasizes that focusing on gender equity within an organization means prioritizing impact over outcome, and viewing Black women through an ecosystem lens and as human beings with potential to contribute to an equitable and inclusive environment.

To break this down, the impact of advancing Black women in the workplace can be viewed through the lens of three perspectives: economic, the workplace and society. The economic perspective highlights how addressing the pay gap for Black women can have a direct impact on their ability to save and invest, leading to greater financial stability and security. The workplace perspective focuses on how creating a more inclusive and equitable environment can lead to increased productivity and innovation. The societal perspective emphasizes how addressing the barriers faced by Black women in the workplace can also tackle issues of anti-Black racism and exploitative femininity.

Gender equity and the issues faced by Black women in the workplace go beyond just addressing the opportunities that White women receive over Black women, but also address the opportunities that other White women receive over women of colour. This comes back to widening the lens and seeking to dismantle more, not fewer, barriers.

The removal of systemic barriers for Black women can have a direct and positive impact on communities, access to education and the ability to participate in the knowledge economy.

When Black women are able to access better-paying jobs, it can help to close the wealth gap and promote economic stability in

Black communities in general. This can lead to increased access to resources and opportunities, such as better housing, healthcare and education. Additionally, Black women often play a vital role in their communities as caregivers, educators and leaders, and when they are able to access better opportunities this can have a ripple effect and positively impact the lives of others in their community.

Systemic barriers such as discrimination in hiring and promotion can limit the ability of Black women to access higher-paying jobs and pursue advanced degrees. However, when these barriers are removed, Black women can have greater access to education, which can lead to better job opportunities and higher earning potential. Additionally, when Black women are able to achieve higher levels of education, they can serve as role models and inspire other Black women to pursue similar paths.

When Black women are able to participate fully and their contributions are recognized it can create a knowledge base and path for other Black women to follow. Black women often bring unique perspectives and experiences to the workforce and their contributions can help to drive innovation and create new opportunities in a variety of fields. Furthermore, when Black women are able to access leadership positions, it can serve as a powerful symbol of inclusivity and equality, and inspire other under-represented groups to see themselves in similar roles.

Black women have historically been under-represented in the workforce and have faced significant barriers to career advancement. However, as Black women are given more opportunities and resources to succeed in the workforce, they can make significant contributions to economic growth. Studies have shown that increasing the representation of women in leadership positions can lead to increased productivity and innovation, and that companies with more diverse leadership teams tend to perform better financially.

The advancement of Black women can lead to a more inclusive and equitable environment for all employees. Black women often bring unique perspectives and experiences to the workplace, and their presence can help to break down stereotypes and promote understanding and empathy among colleagues. Every organization has the opportunity to go above and beyond and that will also lead to wider benefits for all.

A woman's ability to participate in the workforce is also governed by legislation, which is outdated and perpetuates the notion that women are intruders in the workplace. Governments often implement minimum standards, such as minimum wages or anti-discrimination laws, to ensure a basic level of fairness and equity in the workplace. However, these minimum standards do not always guarantee true equity, as they do not address the systemic barriers and power imbalances that can prevent marginalized groups, such as Black women, from accessing equal opportunities and resources.

Your organization can go beyond these minimum standards by implementing internal policies and procedures that actively work to promote equity. This can include creating a culture of inclusivity and understanding, providing resources and support specifically tailored to Black women and committing to diversity and inclusion policies. Organizations can conduct regular audits and evaluations to ensure that their policies and practices are effectively addressing equity and making progress towards creating a more inclusive and equitable work environment.

One example of how an organization can go beyond minimum standards to promote gender equity, specifically related to salary, is by conducting regular salary audits. These audits can help to identify and address disparities in pay between different groups of employees, including Black women.

For instance, the organization can collect data on the salaries of all employees, and then analyze this data to identify any disparities in pay based on factors such as race and gender. If the organization finds that Black women are being paid less than their White or male counterparts, it can take steps to address this pay gap.

Steps in addressing this can be undertaken by doing gender pay gap and/or ethnicity pay gap reporting, as a way to show transparency in acknowledging there is an issue, outlining what steps will be taken to resolve it and also establishing clear guidelines for determining pay levels and rises.

Closing the gap between White and Black women will also close the gap for groups of women who sit in between. In the US, this would work slightly differently as the starting point would be with Latina women.

What this example shows is that by supporting the most marginalized people in an organization, you will help all those in the gap between most and least.

Advancing Black women in the workplace by focusing on gender equity can have a positive impact on the overall success and inclusivity of an organization. Black women have historically been overlooked and under-represented in the workplace, but by broadening the approach and focusing on equity, opportunities can be created for all.

By promoting gender equity and the advancement of Black women, your organization can also demonstrate a commitment to social justice and diversity. This can help to attract and retain top talent and improve the organization's reputation and standing in the community.

In conclusion, advancing Black women in the workplace by focusing on gender equity will not only create opportunities and success for Black women, but will also help to create a more inclusive, resilient and successful organization overall. It's a win-win situation for both your organization and your employees.

CHAPTER THIRTEEN

Making the Theoretical Practical

It may feel overwhelming working where and how to start with the possibly new-to-you contexts and impacts that you have read about so far. This chapter is here to make the theory action-manageable and to help you begin on your gender equity journey or, equally, to find ways to incorporate gender equity into your existing gender equality efforts.

You do not need to have a large contingent of Black women within your organization for it to be a worthwhile exercise. Hopefully, one of the takeaways that you have from the book is the need to focus on impact rather than outcome. Helping one Black woman has a broader impact as it will encourage her managers and colleagues to learn and grow, and it will inform and shape your organization's policies to create a better workplace for any other Black women who will join your organization in the future.

In this chapter, I will walk you through tips on how to deal with exploitative femininity, and how you can use the REASON framework and DARE methodology as a basis for creating equitable changes within your policies, processes and, ultimately, your culture.

I will also walk you through some of the areas in the life cycle of an employee that are overlooked but are critical in establishing gender equity and are supported by the research we carried out for the Experience Chasm Survey 2021 when looking at the experience of Black women in the workplace across Europe.

What is it that Black women would like from their organizations to support their success?

Based on the Experience Chasm Survey 2021, there were clear expectations that Black women had of their employers, some of which were:

1) clear pathways for growth;
2) accountability for racial equity work;
3) equity in pay and also in treatment.

The areas in which Black women saw that their employers were failing them were also clear:

1) Black representation on the executive board;
2) transparency and tangible actions for DEI plans;
3) communication.

How can these issues be overcome?

The answer to this question is through engagement and then through co-creation, but it is hard to engage when organizations have historically ignored and still continue to ignore the needs of Black women within their workforce.

Let's take the first step of engagement.

To create impact, you do not need to have a large community of Black women in your organization. Prioritize long-term success over short-term discomfort. The burden cannot be on the Black woman to show willingness first in order to be supported. Whether you are her direct manager, work in Human Resources or have a bird's-eye view of the organization because of your seniority, there is one clear imperative: you have to be willing to work to engage with her and take the first step.

Many organizations have fallen into the trap of stating that the Black female demographic is too small, which leads to one of two outcomes. Either they group all women of colour together, which, while helpful, still does not address the issues Black women in particular face in terms of both anti-Black racism among other marginalized and minoritized groups and the power hierarchy. Or they justify doing nothing because they cannot see the return on their investment and want to avoid the appearance of giving preferential treatment to one particular group.

Clarity in these situations in both communication and being explicit about what equitable practice is should eliminate 'what about' issues, and should help them to get stuck in.

Having one or very few Black colleagues is a symptom of larger issues, but provides you with some clear indicators:

1) your company has not invested sufficiently in prioritizing Black women;
2) the countdown for being held accountable for the effectiveness or lack thereof of your organization's diversity has begun;
3) this is the perfect time for you to create processes and procedures that are truly embedded in your strategy, which will not only allow your one Black female colleague to thrive, but improve your chances of attracting others and retaining them.

Engagement is not just a simple case of 'We will create an event' or 'We will ask her to lead the Black History Month celebrations'. Real engagement happens when you seek to show the other person that they are valued, that you want to get to know them and that you ultimately want to help them surmount whatever their roadblocks to success are.

Corporate culture has rewarded being transactional with each other for far too long and engaging with a Black woman is no different. This should not just be another task on the list, as the breach of trust between Black women and their employers is exacerbated daily, ranging from having no support to deal with microaggressions to being overlooked for a promotion, and all alongside doing the work.

The expectation cannot be that she will automatically be grateful for the attention; in giving such attention you are centring your own feelings instead of appreciating where she might be in her journey and experience. Depending on your position within the organization, engagement can look a little different.

Managers and senior leadership

Being the only one is a precarious situation, especially as a Black woman. Only too aware of her situation, namely knowing that her behaviour will influence potential future Black employees, there is a natural cautiousness, not to mention the feelings of isolation and being misunderstood, which also compound the fear of speaking out. There is a lot as stake if she speaks out, which can mean that she ends up being in a worse situation than she is already and she does not know you well enough yet to be sure that you are completely trustworthy.

Tip: tread carefully.

Knowing that this is your starting point means that an all-out charm offensive will leave her feeling suspicious, especially if this hasn't been your previous modus operandi.

As with any client, you will have to put in the work to make her feel comfortable. This exercise isn't about her doing the hard work for you and telling you what to do to make things better, but for you to get to know her and find out what her experiences have been.

Before you even think about approaching her, fully acquaint yourself with who she is on paper. How long has she been at the company? What does the feedback on her work say? How has she been compensated in comparison to her White male and female peers? Does her promotion or lack thereof match up to what you would expect based on the feedback she has received during her tenure?

The aim of this is that you can build a picture of her ecosystem in your company.

If the feedback is good, but she still hasn't come forward, does the problem then lie with her manager?

If she does a good job and there is a gender and/or ethnicity wage gap, how has this been missed or are you willing to accept that this has been deliberate, and you will plan to change it?

Once you have identified the issues, ask yourself the question if you think you could have ended up in a similar situation and, if the answer is no, what would have been the main differences?

Could it be that you have a greater freedom to speak out because of your seniority or because you are not the only one? Has it been easier for you because you have a stronger network within the company? Or is quite simply that you don't face either racism or sexism?

The point of this exercise in combination with what you have learned so far will help you better isolate where you can be the most impactful in providing support and also show you where you may experience discomfort, for example if her head of department is a good colleague of yours, but also discriminates against her. This will no doubt be hard for you, but it is the preparation and the forethought that will increase your chances of taking action rather than not.

For her peers: Even if you are not in the position to influence her pay, you are in the position to influence her experience and this is where allyship plays a huge role, too. Take an active interest in where she is excluded: is she in all the project meetings? Are you being invited to more senior meetings, which she has been left out of? This is where you can mention to the organizer either that you will forward it on or that you will bring her because it seems she has been left off. This puts no blame on anyone, but shows that her exclusion has been noted. This action will make all the difference to how she feels about the organization and being seen. Once again, however, just as with any manager or senior leader, the tip is to tread carefully, by letting her know privately that you did this (maybe over a coffee) and, most importantly, why you did it.

Human Resources

The relationship between Human Resources and employees, especially in times of crisis, have been notoriously fraught. *Harvard Business Review*[1] research has shown that there is an

---

[1] https://hbr.org/2022/10/how-hr-lost-employees-trust-and-how-to-get-it-back

inherent distrust of Human Resources and most employees would rather leave an organization than discuss their issues with them. The overwhelming belief is that they only look out for the company rather than the employee and in situations of conflict employees have no chance at all.

One of the scariest experiences a Black woman can have is receiving an unexpected email from Human Resources, so when trying to engage with her your initial focus is to remove the element of fear and surprise.

It is unlikely that she will believe that the conversation is informal, but still be clear when reaching out for a coffee with her that you would like support the senior leader who has taken an interest in her development. Reassure her that there is no issue and explain why you are reaching out to her and not said member of staff. There is nothing wrong with admitting that you are also going on a learning journey.

In your conversation with her, transparency and honesty will make a big difference. Acknowledge the organization's current position and what the aims are and, most importantly, what this could have to do with her, if she would like to be involved.

Respecting her journey means accepting the fact that she may not want to be a part of it because she cannot see the benefits and because she does not want to put herself in the position of being visible and under scrutiny.

Leave the door open for her to always be able to follow up with you, but do not exert pressure. This will no doubt be a new position for her to be in, so the focus comes back to impact over speed of change.

Coming prepared to listen, if she wants to open up, is crucial and, if it is clear that there is no way she will tell you more, there are two possibilities. One is to seek external help and the other is to ask her if she would prefer you to connect her with the member of staff directly.

Whether you are her manager or you sit in Human Resources, when trying to build a relationship, avoid overselling the benefits of her involvement, especially when there is no broader plan and you have not considered the ways she needs to be protected. The ultimate plan is to help her, but it should not come at the price of her being pressured into it.

Always remember: Black women are used to hearing about so many new company initiatives that are meant to be beneficial for women, but they have often yet to see any changes in their daily lives.

It is easy to believe that because you have a gender-based initiative you have done enough. The default is to ask her 'Is she sure that she doesn't want to be part of the DEI initiative?' If she displays hesitation, it confirms that the timing is not yet right for her to be openly involved, but it does not take away the opportunity to collaborate and co-create. Highlighting the importance of her contribution is key to being able to move forward.

Part of your outreach is for you to learn what it means to sit at the intersection of being Black and a woman and to understand what exactly is missing for her in the workplace. It is key that she remains at the forefront of your mind. This is not about undermining your leadership (if you are her manager) but, rather, sharpening it.

You may feel defensive and want to sell all that you have already done, but in not accepting the feedback she gives, exactly as she describes it, you run the risk of not making any meaningful changes and also pushing her into the position of having to contemplate her next move. This may be to leave the company because she doesn't feel that there will be any positive changes for her in the future.

This first step of reaching out will put you on the path to equitable actions, as you learn to centre others, become an ally and, in doing so, provide your sole Black female colleague with the opportunity to thrive.

The difficulty can sometimes come in knowing how to strike the balance between burdening her and working together and this is where the principles of co-creation are so useful.

In the book *You Are Your Best Thing*, an anthology of the Black experience in the US co-edited by Brené Brown and Tarana Burke, there was a very powerful statement in the prologue: Brené Brown said that 'lived experience is more important than academic or theoretical experience'.

This statement reiterates the importance of amplifying the experiences and voices of those who are oppressed, particularly in the context of gender equity. The key driver that differentiates her being burdened from her providing input is that a strategic element should also be incorporated. Simply put, she should be able to provide input without being asked to craft the solution.

Your ability to accept that anecdotes are also data will change the path of the interaction with her. Anecdotes provide deeper insights and reveal more than a straightforward question-and-answer exchange. They are an opportunity to explore the nuance of someone's experience.

In the case of Black women facing challenges to their credibility, the anecdotes they give are not analyzed in the way they should be and are seen as being gossip as opposed to the truth. Her anecdotes will no doubt challenge your experiences, but that does not make them any less true. It is in accepting them that you create opportunity.

The combination of lived and academic experience gives rise to the possibilities of co-creation; to find a solution that serves Black women, but also serves the needs of the business.

The overarching label of diversity and inclusion has managed to distance from us the reality that behind this injustice there is lived experience. That the voices of those who have been historically and systemically muted need to be switched on to accelerate making inroads into an area that might resemble success.

The problem is that academic or theoretical know-how comes with a prestige and respect that is not afforded to the oppressed who share their lived experience to enable their companies to find or create a solution.

Once shared, however, their experiences are commonly dismissed as useless because of the discomfort they cause and are then compared less favourably to the academic experience, which leaves leaders feeling better but fails to help the women.

Co-creation can be critical in moving this dial, involving a combination of giving the right weight to lived experience and combining it with technical knowledge and strategic capability to get to this outcome of equity.

A lot of companies have made the mistake of overleveraging those with lived experience by not only asking them to share their stories, but also expecting them to be able to deliver a strategic plan and provide the solution.

The question then is: how much are companies really asking Black women to do?

Asking them to participate and help with diversity and inclusion initiatives is one thing, but are they also being asked to provide and define what the solutions should be, all as an add-on to their job?

This isn't to say that those who have lived experiences don't have strategic capabilities, but, rather, that a company's success is also based on selecting the right candidates for the right roles. Namely, being clear on who is providing strategic or academic experience and who is providing lived experience, outlining the objectives of both their roles and providing more than adequate support.

Sharing experiences of racial trauma is a very different experience from being able to objectively discuss racism through a looking glass. Since George Floyd's murder, many companies have asked Black colleagues to share their stories, but have asked non-Black service providers to create solutions.

This has created tension, as the burden has been on Black colleagues to do more emotional heavy lifting to be seen and heard to help some service providers understand the gravity of their situation. The most tragic part is that they have also failed to solve the issues Black colleagues have faced.

Lived experience should take priority not just at the point of storytelling, but throughout the whole process of building solutions together and not in a bubble. Without lived experience in the room, there can be a trivialization of the topic, a shying away from what is uncomfortable and awkward.

When the distance from the problem is too great, the chances of forgetting that people live this trauma day in and day out increase. We have to talk to understand the problems. It is crucial to have the right people in the room, those who have lived experiences and perspectives that can provide valuable insights and solutions. This includes not only marginalized and minoritized groups, but also those who have the power and authority to make changes within the organization. Without their active participation and commitment, progress will be limited. It is also important to remember that these conversations and solutions should not be one-off or short-term, but an ongoing process of continuous improvement and accountability.

It is possible to find solutions that serve both the uplifting of the women and the strategic goals of the company. However, doing so will take listening and learning and accepting that failure is part of the journey to success.

There are two categories of action that will assist you on your journey. One is detection and the other is proactivity.

As discussed throughout this book, not all the barriers are easy to detect, and some require proactivity to gain the trust of Black women within your organization in order to get to the root of the issue.

Exploitative femininity is one of those behaviours that will take more time to be detected and observed. The meticulous execution together with the strategy that has been implemented can catch even the more astute of us off guard. It works on the premise of gaslighting – that you are never quite sure what is really true – and this is why it is critical that not only you but others in your team are aware of this kind of behaviour.

How can you protect yourself and others?

Warning: an employee who becomes a victim of exploitative femininity will suffer an array of negative feelings, often insecurity, self-doubt, disbelief, isolation and powerlessness. Left unaddressed, the situation and the feelings it engenders can eventually lead to a state of personal and professional paralysis. The antidote is to arm yourself in advance with the knowledge you need to spot the presence and danger of exploitative femininity, analyze the situation, gather allies and create an affirming strategy in response.

Insecurity naturally arises in the face of exploitative femininity. The insidious nature of the offence creates a reasonable worry that no one will believe the Black woman's story, especially if she is new to the office. She may come to you to tell you about the existence of a campaign against her and you may refuse to acknowledge it.

Firstly, when she tells you about the campaign, before you decide that it cannot be true, take a step back and ask for more details. Without your support or that of others, the situation will begin to escalate.

With no one in her corner, she will probably feel powerless to change the dynamics. The feeling of isolation will begin, and it will be entirely intentional. The exploiter knows that as long as her target feels alone she is easier to manipulate, and that it is also easier to manipulate others' opinions of her.

Dismantling exploitative femininity will be uncomfortable for a lot of people; a team of one is probably powerless but even one ally drastically changes the odds. As an ally, you can help her begin difficult conversations and force transparency. (The other options she will be left with are variations of severance, whether she is pushed out or decides to leave of her own accord.)

The insecurity begets self-doubt. Maybe you have misconstrued the behaviour of a colleague. How could the 'nice' one, who was first to welcome you and invite you for coffee or lunch, actually be responsible for the situation? You may wonder whether you're reading too much into the words and actions of someone generally believed to be quite pleasant. Worse, you might begin to question your own ability to discern the reality of a situation or your judgement regarding others.

Transforming the conversation from gossip to honest confrontation of existing exploitation will require persistence, follow-up and documentation. Instead of whispered chats in the corridor, it's time for emails that clarify behaviours and their context. It will require the whole team of colleagues to think more deeply and to express themselves more astutely, especially when they are on the record. As a bonus, the exploiter will know that others are involved. It will become progressively more difficult for her to twist the meaning and context of her words and actions or blame others for what she will likely term 'mistaken' perceptions.

All this can generate disbelief, fuelled by the classic office power tool, gossip. In an attempt to validate your understanding of the exploitative femininity being used to undermine you, it's natural to ask around a bit, to see whether things are as obvious as they seem to you. Unfortunately, most of your colleagues, either unaware or just unwilling to become entangled in the drama, will push back and try to convince you that you are over-reacting, or taking the exploiter's words and actions out of context. There may be the occasional excuse-maker willing to acknowledge the issue while insisting that the offender doesn't really mean what she is saying. If you are really fortunate, you will find a potential ally who sees and understands the trap you're in.

Pushing through barriers of group perception and asking direct questions that require direct answers within the framework of a professional setting effectively corners the aggressor. She will have two choices: to begin creating ever more elaborate lies to cover her exploitative behaviour, or to drop the charade and become openly aggressive. The truth will out: other people will no longer be able to ignore her behaviour. The purpose of this should never be forgotten, which is protecting your Black female colleague, leading the way towards a more open, inclusive workplace.

In defending yourself and your colleagues, you will have undoubtedly reached greater clarity about what constitutes a healthy work culture, and what you need and want. What your responsibilities are as a leader and colleagues. You have also set an example. Standing together with your Black female colleague will help to build a mutually beneficial and true professional alliance among women that can withstand and replace the mythical sisterhood that currently disguises so much dysfunction.

Now let's look at how the REASON framework can support your efforts.

REASON framework

The REASON framework was created off the back of the Experience Chasm Survey 2021 and the work I did with several organizations. The REASON framework comprises principles that drive actions that any company can take to ensure it retains and engages Black women.

The principles behind the REASON framework work on the premise that while you may not yet have begun your journey, you will be able to apply the framework using this book as a reference and guide. REASON is a framework that can work alongside your existing gender equality efforts and serve as an enhancement. Using the REASON framework does not mean that you have to start from the beginning.

REASON helps you remove the burden from Black women to provide solutions and also empowers organizations to remove the institutional barriers that prevent Black women from thriving.

Gender equality has shown what works for women and gender equity refines that proposition.

The Experience Chasm Survey 2021 showed that Black women are more than ready to share their experiences if the information will positively impact Black women as a whole within their organization. More than 50 per cent of respondents felt that the largest impact to their progress was the knowledge gaps of senior leadership and their managers, and the fact that they had not taken the time to fill them.

The framework is designed to help organizations remove institutional barriers and create a more inclusive and equitable environment for Black women, but it can only be effective when leaders are willing to challenge their assumptions and lean into the discomfort that comes with changing the status quo. Inclusive leadership and an inclusive culture require a willingness to question the way things have always been done and to embrace new perspectives and ways of doing things. This means being open to feedback and input from employees, especially Black women, and being willing to make changes to policies, practices and culture in order to create a more equitable and inclusive environment in the workplace.

Leaders must be willing to take responsibility for creating an inclusive culture and take active steps to address any unconscious bias or discrimination and to foster an environment in which all employees feel valued and respected. This requires active listening, empathy and a willingness to continuously learn and adapt. Inclusive leadership is not a one-off; it's an ongoing process of learning, growing and adapting. The REASON framework is a tool to support that process.

The REASON framework is designed to be scalable and can be applied to organizations of any size. The principles of the framework focus on inclusive leadership and equitable practices, and can be used to amplify the voices and experiences of Black women in order to accelerate solutions and identify bottlenecks in the pipeline. It takes a critical look at the organization's current state, identifying areas of strength and areas that need improvement, and engaging employees.

It's important to note that the application of the framework may look different depending on the size of an organization, but the principles remain the same. Smaller organizations may have fewer resources but they can still work on the same principles and create a culture of equity. In larger organizations, more resources and a more structured approach may be required to implement the changes, but the goal is still the same: to create an equitable and inclusive environment for Black women.

The REASON framework in action

Recognition, Engagement, Action, Support, Outreach, Navigation

Recognition: how you recognize a symptom to find the root of the issue that is preventing gender equity practice? Symptoms can show up in four key areas:

1) Pay disparities: where do Black women sit when it comes to the gender and ethnicity pay gap?
2) Representation: from what levels of seniority are Black women noticeably absent?
3) Promotion: what are the progression rates of Black women in comparison to their peers?
4) Harassment: what percentage of harassment or discrimination cases have been reported by Black women and how many of those have led to a departure?

There are a lot of widely acknowledged 'problems' that are a symptom. Examples of symptoms are:

- not being enough talent or qualified talent;
- Black women do not apply;
- we don't really know her.

For each of these problems, the question is why? What needs to change in process or culture?

When there is not enough talent or qualified talent, who made the decision about who was appropriate? Who was the first touch point within the organization to receive the CV? Who wrote the job criteria? If it was an internal job posting, what is the gender balance of the existing team and what could the impact be on the job description? Where are you looking for candidates?

Taking the example of promotions:

Is there transparency in the process? When looking at the reasons why Black women are not progressing within your organization, have you analyzed who was in the interview panel? Was there transparent feedback about why they were not promoted?

Asking some of these questions will quickly reveal where the problem with some of the processes lies and will also help identify which teams in the business may need more support. This may be the hiring manager, just as much as it might be someone in Human Resources.

There two important elements when looking at gender equity: the experience of Black women and the experience of their peers. One does not invalidate the other, but it is through being able to see the gaps in their experiences that you will also be able to close them.

Action: workplace culture audits, both on a small team and all the way to an entire organization, can provide you with a complete picture of where you can have the largest positive impact for Black women. Taking both a top-down and bottom-up approach will also help you find the source of your issues. Is there a disparity between what is being said at the top and what is trickling down in the middle?

Engagement: building trust and providing both psychological and physical safety.

Some strategies for building trust and creating a safe environment include:

- establishing clear policies and procedures for reporting harassment and discrimination based on gender and race;
- encouraging open and honest communication and actively listening to concerns and feedback from employees;

- providing resources and support for individuals who have experienced harassment or discrimination.

Engaging with a Black woman in your organization should not happen exclusively when there are issues and you need her help. It should be a continuous process that involves taking a litmus test to see if she can progress, as well as whether or not there is the potential to improve existing processes.

For example, if she has just gone through the promotion process, whether she has got the job or not, this would be the opportune moment to get her feedback on the process. How did she find the interview panel? Was there clear and timely communication? If she was not successful in getting the job, did she receive clear feedback and is it also clear where she would need to make improvements?

The purpose of engagement should show value, not just because she is a Black woman but because you value her expertise and contribution. Engagement is driven by the feeling of belonging and being seen.

The Experience Chasm Survey 2021 showed that 60 per cent of the respondents were overlooked by being missed off invitations for strategic meetings, which shows neither care nor consideration and creates another gap in trust and the feeling of belonging.

These are also ways that you can ensure she feels seen and heard. There does not always have to be a specific initiative to drive more engagement with and from her; it can just be as simple as ensuring that she is not missed off important meetings and, if she has been, that she is updated as soon as possible by the organizer and not by a third party.

Action: be clear on how and why you are taking action.

There are stages to taking action and not all can happen at once, but the most important group to the success of any changes you want to make are the C-suite and executive committee teams. Without their buy-in and support it will be very difficult or even impossible to make long-lasting changes.

After getting feedback and a complete view, it is just as important to present these teams with a strategy as well as a case for why gender equity is critical for your organization.

Who within the organization needs training, and what could be the potential impact of this initiative? Does it mean that certain seniority levels need to do some training on inclusive leadership, racial equity and gender equity?

Do you need to build new criteria around promotion criteria and job description process? Do HR need support, too, with issues around intersectionality?

When these initiatives begin, the most difficult part will be communication, but this underscores your organization's commitment to transparency, which builds trust and also leads to change.

It is not possible to do everything at the same time, but in analyzing your feedback and surveys, there will be clear themes that develop. Plotting satisfaction over tenure with gender and race will give you a good indication of who is most 'at risk', that is who is most likely to leave at this point in their career. The inclination may be to focus on other areas of the business that directly have profit and loss attached to them, but focusing on this 'at risk' group should be viewed as an investment, even if the benefits take longer to appear.

Support: addressing both intended and unintended consequences of change.

Prioritizing gender equity within your organization will have both intended and unintended consequences, which means recognizing that support will be needed both for Black women and for others.

Why is it important to consider other groups when focusing on Black women?

There will be two groups of people – supporters and detractors – and both require attention, even if to a differing degree. It is easy to say that detractors can simply be ignored, but the opposite is true. They will still need to be managed, so that they don't obstruct progress.

Support must go hand-in-hand with an overarching strategy. There is no point in having workshops here and there if the information being imparted in them bears no relation to what you are trying achieve.

The first step is socializing and mainstreaming gender equity as an integral part of your organization's overall DEI and ESG strategy with emphasis on how gender equity and racial equity concerns impact everyone.

Action:

- training managers about the benefits of gender equity and racial equity and holding them accountable for the implementation of the organization's policies;
- developing gender equity training for recruiters within the organization, those responsible for making promotion decisions, and line managers and those who authorize or create career development opportunities.

There is the other side of the equation that is often forgotten. While you are on your journey, your organization is not quite where it should be for a Black woman to thrive, so she will need external as well as internal support while she moves through the organization. This can take many forms, including some suggestions made earlier (with caveats), such as mentorship, sponsorship and career development programmes.

One of the most valuable resources she could have access to is an executive coach, even if she is not yet an executive, or even a coach as a sounding board who has the lived experience and the expertise to meaningfully support her and help to ease some of her burden.

Outreach: making positive changes now to support the workforce of the future.

It might seem out of place to see outreach as part of the framework, but the incoming generation are a very important part of your organization, just as much as the role your organization plays within communities.

When trying to create an equitable and inclusive organization, it is just as important to connect with and understand the needs of the next generation, who are very aware of their needs and wants, as it is those of the current generation.

This goes further than future employees; it concerns learning about the challenges, but also finding ways to give back. Working with grassroots organizations, charities and communities will also help you to close the gap of gender inequity. Deepen your learning so that you can put gender equity into practice. This will have the positive effect of encouraging the next generation to work for you, and for them to also see that there are real opportunities for progression within an organization that recognizes and is actively working to dismantle the barriers to success. Taking this approach will also confirm that you are an organization that's as much focused on today as on the future.

Some strategies for outreach include:

- partnering with organizations that support individuals from under-represented genders, such as professional associations or diversity and inclusion groups;
- participating in job fairs and other recruitment events that focus on diversity;
- developing internship and mentorship programmes to help individuals from under-represented groups gain experience and build connections within the industry.

Navigation: adapting and measuring your progress.

Accelerating gender equity is dynamic and will require navigation as your organization evolves. Creating the space for measurement in progress will be vital, as well as your organization's ability to pivot to respond to both the intended and unintended consequences of driving change within your culture.

Some strategies for navigation include:

- providing resources and support to help individuals understand and access the organization's policies and procedures;
- establishing clear channels of communication and actively listening to the concerns and feedback of employees.

Without regular monitoring and the follow-up of actions and initiatives, it cannot be properly seen whether actions have been beneficial or may require variation in the future.

The definition of success must be a combination of the needs of Black women and the needs of the organization. If it only serves one of these groups, then it will be even more difficult to achieve anything.

When setting goals, you must ensure that they are not aspirational, but are kept within realistic boundaries. They should also be relevant to achieving gender equity.

Taking the promotion process as an example: if the aim is to have a better process based on feedback, then it might mean implementing new training for recruiters within the business and getting feedback from Black women again, and then seeing if there is an improvement.

Action:

- use peer benchmarking to do more regular checks on employee satisfaction levels;
- assess over time if the goals that you set are realistic and achievable.

The REASON framework for gender equity can be further supported by the DARE methodology of Diagnose, Assess, Recalibrate and Embed.

The DARE methodology will help your organization to take a systematic approach to addressing issues of diversity, equity, and inclusion (DEI), specifically gender and racial equity. The steps of the DARE methodology are as follows:

Diagnose: this step involves identifying and understanding the root causes of the issues relating to DEI within the organization. This can involve collecting and analyzing data, consulting with experts and engaging with employees by means of surveys and focus groups.

Assess: this step involves evaluating the current policies, practices and culture of the organization in order to determine how they may contribute to the issues identified in the diagnosis step.

Recalibrate: this step involves taking action to address the issues identified in the previous steps. This may involve revising policies and procedures, developing new programmes and initiatives and providing training and resources.

Embed: this step involves ensuring that the solutions and strategies are fully integrated into the organization's culture, policies and practices and continuously monitored to ensure their effectiveness and sustainability.

The DARE methodology is a structured approach to implementing the REASON framework, which provides a roadmap for addressing issues of gender equity in an organization. Each step of the methodology is designed to guide organizations through the process of creating a more equitable and inclusive environment for Black women. The DARE methodology is a cyclical process, and it is important to understand that it is not a one-time event. Organizations should be continuously monitoring, evaluating and recalibrating their efforts to ensure long-term success and progress.

The REASON framework will support you as you craft a gender equity strategy and you can use the checklist below to help you define the parameters and how they can be measured.

Outcomes: what is the direct benefit of this initiative to Black women within your organization?	
Impact: what could be the impact of this initiative beyond this demographic?	

Peer benchmarking: have you compared the experiences of Black women, White women and women of colour within your organization? And can you clearly address the gap?	
Alignment to business strategy: does this initiative align with overall business strategy and is it strong enough to get senior leader and executive committee buy-in?	
Timeframe/budget: have you set a realistic timeframe and budget to implement this initiative?	
Data: is there enough quantitative and qualitative data or even anecdotal data to support the need for this initiative?	
Success metrics: have Black women been a part of determining success metrics? Have you built success metrics for other groups? Have you determined intervals and methods of measurement?	
Realistic: have you set realistic goals that can be achieved within the timeframe set?	

The REASON framework encapsulates the importance of finding the root of the problems, removing the burden from Black women to find solutions, how to build trust from leaders to their team members and back, increased satisfaction and using the feeling of belonging to increase productivity. It also impacts above the group you are trying to help and gives a focus on how to meaningfully start on this journey.

The emphasis on REASON is to be a guide for employers to consider as we move more into a climate of increased accountability regulation, but also with a focus in the shift in the future of work and how that impacts Black women. The shift that we are currently experiencing requires extra attention be paid to the policies and processes that perpetuate gender equity.

The framework provides you with concrete steps to enable you to address gender inequity, but also to educate yourself and others on the broader context of racism and sexism within the workplace. The structure is intended to make an overwhelming topic manageable and provide you with the support and confidence to try and try again.

I continue to learn that failure is part of success but it still feels unpleasant. The hardest thing to do sometimes is to stop our perfectionism paralyzing us. It feels easier to keep planning than to move to the implementation phase, for fear of getting it wrong, but the danger is that when Black women cannot see action within your organization, they can only believe what they see or, rather, do not see. I hope that reading this book has emboldened you to talk more about gender equity and to dig further into your organization's culture as your radar will now be even more finely attuned. I hope you will feel emboldened to ask those pointed questions, such as why has it been impossible to recruit Black women, and if anyone has looked into it further rather than just making the statement.

Closing the Gap is not designed to make you an activist, but to help you to critically approach what you are asking of Black women in your organization. Are you setting them up for success or failure? What are the ways that you can improve? What have been the results of gender equality initiatives; that is, how many Black women have also been promoted as part of the increase in female representation in leadership?

I hope this book also serves as a reminder that equity takes time and that even though the countdown is underway, as people want to see results, laying strong foundations and putting in the extra work of education, process analysis and setting realistic but also reasonable timeframes will drive long-lasting and sustainable gender equity within your organization.

Appendix: Further Thoughts

There are some small yet impactful changes that you can make before you start to dig into the bigger issues. Here are a few that I would like to share, which may help you start your journey on the path to gender equity.

I will take key moments in the life cycle of an employee to address them:

The interview process

Sadly, the interview process is still very predatory in its design and for some the opportunity to sit on an interview panel gives them the opportunity to trip people up, which should not be the aim at all.

How can the interview process be equitable?

On the side of the interviewers, there are several things that should be done. The selection of the interview panel should be reviewed by HR and a decision-maker. Are all the members of the panel relevant to the process and do they have a known opinion on gender and racial equity?

Set up a meeting to discuss the criteria of nice-to-haves and must-haves. In my experience with internal recruiters, when challenged, almost 50 per cent of the job criteria that are listed as a must-have are in fact a nice-to-have. Discuss what the basis of these criteria is. If this has been based on a male-dominated team, then the job description requirements will be skewed towards men.

Ask yourself questions such as:

- Have all the panel participated in racial equity and gender equity training to be able to recognize the behaviours that will display bias? Do you have this kind of training?
- Have you created structured interview questions, so that you can compare answers like for like, as opposed to who your favourite was, from a cultural fit perspective? We are all inclined to affinity bias. However, creating standardized questions will help you reduce it when looking at the answers.
- Are you collecting data on the demographics of your interview pool and the candidates who are offered jobs, and using this data to identify any potential issues of bias or inequity?

The decision process is also an important milestone. Each panellist doing their rankings alone and then coming together to discuss them is a better way to decide than having one more senior voice dictate their favourite and everyone else falling into line.

Finally, interviews should be about setting your candidate up for success. That means sending them the profiles of the panellists along with the expertise they have and why they are joining the process. Give them the opportunity to do their due diligence before the interview.

After getting the job, the next contact point for most employees is their first day, but there is more you can do to encourage a sense of belonging and value.

This is what is called the pre-onboarding process, something I learned about from a client.

Before the first day, make sure you put in a call or ask the most senior person in the team to congratulate and welcome them. This is a small act that has a lot of impact in showing that they are not just a number but are being seen.

Creating a connection before the first day will also increase their anticipation, which means that them having a positive first day is even more important.

The onboarding process

The first day for nearly everyone is filled with fear, excitement and anticipation. I think every new joiner asks themselves whether they have made the right decision, if they will fit in, if the job they accepted is the job they will be doing.

It may be easy to forget, but the first day is not about the new joiner living up to expectations, but for you to confirm that they have made the right choice.

This is the moment of opportunity for you to start as you mean to go on and build the feeling of belonging.

Things to consider before they get there are:

- Can their entry pass be organized before they start and, if so, is it ready?
- Is there someone available to meet them when they arrive?
- Has their computer log-in been sorted out?

Or do they arrive to chaos? Do they have to wait around for someone to stop working to remember they are there, so that they can be shown around and be included?

The first day and the onboarding process are an opportunity for companies to sell what they offered on their side. Interview processes in many cases also create a sense of nostalgia about the best times in the company, but is that still reflected in the day-to-day?

Inclusion is not defined by all the bells and whistles; it can also just be about the small things.

The onboarding process is not just the responsibility of HR and the hiring manager. Every person on the new starter's team needs to be made aware of their responsibility and should embrace it, so that she also does not feel as though she is an inconvenience or an unnecessary distraction.

The questions that need constantly to be asked by every individual are: have I done enough to make my new colleague feel welcome or have I put the onus on them to take the first step?

What role can I play to help affirm that they are a welcome member of the team?

It has to go further than sending out a blast email announcing that a new person has joined and where they sit. More importantly, the sort of welcome each person receives should not be based on their seniority.

Some people like to have a big welcome; others prefer to keep things low key. Centring a Black woman's needs means taking her guidance as to how she would like to be introduced.

She may feel shy or nervous about being the first or only Black woman. She might want to observe a little before a blast email goes out. She is aware of her position and profile and you will be able to help her navigate that by talking to her, rather than just doing the standard onboarding.

There is so much to think about when it comes to the onboarding process and it shouldn't be taken lightly.

There shouldn't be a perfunctory mill that each person is run through, but, rather, a carefully considered programme that is put together. Onboarding is not just about orientation and paperwork, it's also an opportunity to set the tone for how new employees will be treated and integrated into the organization. A well-designed onboarding programme can set new employees up for success and help them feel more connected to the company's mission and values.

Some of the tips I would recommend include:

1) Don't overlook the importance of the first day, so go above and beyond the minimum requirements.
2) Create a community; create a cohort. Even if there doesn't seem to be an easy way to create it, work harder at it with Human Resources.
3) Train managers to go above and beyond to create a safety net, to provide introductions. To understand the long- and short-term benefits of this approach. Make this a key part of the cultural responsibility of any manager – not just to send out emails, but to be part of the introductory meetings.

This is how you can start to create a strong foundation. Once you belong, you are willing to do more and you feel more satisfied. Not only that, but you work together with others more cohesively.

It's not for the new person always to have to put themselves out there. A new person has already put the hard work in; now is the time for the company to fully invite them into the culture.

When you invite someone in, you should take the lead in helping them navigate, understand and be successful in order to make sure that they feel as though they belong.

If you don't know if your company has an onboarding process, now is the time to find out, as it presents an opportunity to create one.

Your goal should be to make sure that every person who walks through your door feels a part of your business and welcomed and that is done by taking the time to consider what is important on the first day.

Inclusion starts from right from the onboarding stage and is critical to your culture. It is the perfect moment to share your values and make sure that your new joiners sees that you live the company values.

It is also important to note that inclusion is not just about making new hires feel welcome. It is also about creating an environment where all employees feel as if they belong, regardless of their background or identity.

This will also give you the opportunity to show the new employee how the organization lives its values.

There should be no pressure for her to get involved, but it never hurts to talk about what initiatives there are in general but also specifically for Black women.

She may not react, as it is the first day, but it is a bonus that she is then informed and can make a decision on how she chooses to engage with initiatives going forward.

The update/check-in process

When you have a new joiner, the regular update meetings happen without any effort. You are naturally interested to hear how she is acclimatizing, finding her way around systems and getting to know people.

However, these regular update meetings tend to taper off once you have made the decision that she should be settled by now. I can remember being a part of these conversations, and then after the first month a new joiner was left to fend for themselves and fell into the same routine as everyone else of having task-based update meetings.

A better way to help her settle in is to keep these regular meetings going for six months but for them to be focused on her wellbeing as well as her job. She may not be willing to divulge her concerns at the beginning because she still needs to get to know you, but making her wellbeing a consistent topic and showing her that you are interested in her as a person, not just as a function, will not only help build trust, but also increase her feeling of being valued.

Normalizing conversations around wellbeing will also have a positive effect on the team of developing an open, collegiate atmosphere. By encouraging open communication about mental and physical health, organizations can foster a culture of caring and understanding.

Fifty-seven per cent of the respondents in the Experience Chasm Survey 2021 stated that outside of the yearly appraisal they had no extra update meetings with their managers and that was also a stated reason why they felt overlooked.

Development within an organization should not only be seen through the lens of leadership and skills enhancements, but also through her ability to develop a sense of belonging in your organization. The 'E' in the REASON framework is engagement and these update meetings are the perfect moment to foster this; the opportunity for you to be informed about difficult situations ranging from exploitative femininity to feelings of isolation.

The importance of these meetings and the opportunity for exchange and relationship building cannot be overstated.

Pay review conversations

Black women are the second lowest-paid group in the US, and in the UK, Black women are the lowest paid.[1]

Having her pay review conversation is not just about delivering a number and expecting her to be happy with it, but for you to be sure that the pay rise she is being given is an equitable one.

Black women are consistently short-changed, meaning that their pay rises do not close the gaps, but keep her at a disadvantage, irrespective of how much she earns. The question is, is she paid the same as her colleagues, doing the same job, all factors considered including years of service, performance evaluations and level of experience?

The work is in the research and addressing the pay gaps before meeting with her to try to move the dial. This will mean working with HR to get them to provide you with data, so that you can analyze the pay structures and grades. Are there identifiable patterns or disparities in pay, considering factors such as job function, level of experience and performance, that make her gender and ethnicity the only two reasons why she would be on a different pay grade?

Ensuring equitable pay will have a significant impact on your organization as well as on the women. The positive effects of being transparent about pays gaps, and seeking to close them by providing fair and equal pay, can improve employee morale and motivation, as well as increasing engagement and retention.

In addition, it can help to reduce staff turnover, as she will be less likely to leave if she feels that she is being paid fairly.

---

[1] https://www.ons.gov.uk/employmentandlabourmarket/peopleinwork/earningsandworkinghours/datasets/ethnicitypaygapreferencetables

Your organization will be seen as being credible and genuine if it supports gender equity in both word and deed. Equitable pay will have a positive impact on your organization's reputation and bottom line, as both clients and shareholders will view your organization more favourably if you are seen to be taking action against pay inequity. Ultimately, ensuring equitable pay is an important step that your organization can take to create a more inclusive and equitable work environment, and can bring benefits to all the stakeholders of the organization.

I call it the circle of money: a woman's ability to earn money dictates her ability to save and to invest. Paying her equitably also means giving her the opportunity to create opportunities for others outside the organization.

According to the Organisation for Economic Co-operation and Development (OECD),[2] 'Women typically invest a higher proportion of their earnings in their families and communities than men.'

This principle underscores the importance of pay equity and why even if you only have one Black woman within your organization, the impact can be greater than you realize.

Promotion process and pathways

All the respondents in the Experience Chasm Survey 2021 stated 100 per cent that their organizations were failing them when it came to providing clear pathways for growth and development.

---

[2]https://www.oecd.org/dac/gender-development/investinginwomenandgirls.htm

When working with an individual to plot out their career path, it is important to recognize that there is no one-size-fits-all solution. Every employee has unique career aspirations, goals and experiences. However, it is nevertheless possible to define some factors that may help her to have a better understanding of her career trajectory.

One approach is to look at the trajectories of other colleagues who started out at the same level as the employee. This can provide a sense of what the typical career path looks like within the organization, and can help her to identify the milestones, skills and experiences that are typically associated with advancement.

Another approach is to identify the skills, experiences and competencies that are required for the roles the employee is interested in, and to work with her to map out a plan that will help her acquire them. This can help the employee understand what specific steps she can take to develop the knowledge and skills that she needs to progress in her career.

It is also essential to discuss with the employee what her career aspirations are, and help her to identify her long-term career goals, then align her short-term development opportunities with the long-term aspirations.

It is important to remember that career development plans should be flexible, and should be reviewed and updated regularly, based on the employee's performance, the organization's needs and the industry development.

There is no expectation that a career path should be prescriptive; it's still possible to define some factors that can help the employee have a better picture of their trajectory. By looking at the trajectories of other colleagues, identifying the skills and competencies required for the roles they aspire to and aligning them with the employee's aspirations, the employee will have more clarity and a firmer goal.

Career development and growth is an important aspect of any job and your organization probably has a title hierarchy in place to provide a sense of structure and direction for employees. Typically, this hierarchy starts with entry-level positions such as analyst or associate, and progresses through intermediate roles such as director and managing director, each with an estimated timeframe for advancement and specific milestones to be achieved along the way.

However, it is important to note that this type of hierarchical structure may not be suitable for everyone. For example, some individuals may have different career aspirations and may not wish to progress through the traditional hierarchy. That's why it's crucial for you to create a personalized career development plan to support her goals and aspirations.

Another way to assist her in plotting out her career path is to help her identify potential growth opportunities within the organization, and provide guidance and resources leveraging your access to information and network. This can include training programmes, specific skills-based courses and other opportunities to gain new skills and experiences.

Additionally, providing regular performance evaluations and feedback can help employees understand their strengths and areas for improvement, identify the milestones that need to be accomplished to move up the ladder and understand the expectations for their role.

In summary, a title hierarchy can provide a sense of structure and direction for employees, but it's crucial to remember that not everyone may want to or can move up the traditional ladder, so identifying where there could be roadblocks is just as crucial to a personalized career development plan as supporting her goals and aspirations. Clear guidance and support, and regular feedback, can help the employee to understand her career path, milestones, and how she can accomplish them, and just as with starting in the organization, this will reinforce her commitment as she see that she is valued.

Promotions are not guaranteed but having a clear understanding of the qualifications and markers that are required for advancement can help her better prepare for them.

Even in instances where she is unsuccessful at being promoted, there is still an opportunity to create value. Feedback is the most valuable resource and working together with her is a more productive way to help her achieve her promotion in the future.

Your role is to empower your employee with the right skills and experiences to be prepared and to increase their chances of promotion, while breaking down the barriers that obstruct her path to success.

My final words

I wrote this book as a dedication to Black women in the workplace. As a Black woman, I understand that all too often our willingness to be a part of the solution is exploited and we are expected to have all the solutions.

I did not want to write a book that asked Black women to fix themselves, but to write a guide to show organizations how much more they can do enable our further success.

Closing the Gap is just as relevant for CEOs as it is to Human Resources, or for any individual in an organization. I wanted to give context to why the concept of meritocracy does not work when you are Black woman. To add nuance to the ideas of sponsorship and mentorship and discuss what extra support is needed for sponsors and mentors to effectively do their job for Black women.

I wanted you to be able to go on a journey that highlights the construct of the workplace and the positioning of Black women as intruders, but also what the impact of inaction is. This book is also a call to action to highlight the urgency of focusing on gender equity within your organization, as its impact, like that of racial equity, is not just confined to the workplace.

I also hope that *Closing the Gap* has shed light on some situations where you could not articulate what was wrong, and that now you have a clearer vision.

My hope for Black women is that you feel seen and heard and that I have done justice to our experiences, and that you can use this book as a guide for your managers and colleagues.

I also hope for any reader that you feel empowered to speak up and share what you have learned here, too, and that you can take these tips and put them into practice.

Acknowledgements

I don't remember who said it, but there's a saying that goes 'We don't achieve things alone, but with the help of others', and even though my name is on the cover, so many people have supported me, encouraged me and inspired me to take this step.

The first person I want to thank is my mum, Norma Golding.

We are all a product of our upbringing and I'm thankful for mine. She instilled a strong sense of self and self-confidence, which allowed me to love being a Black woman. She taught me the importance of sharing and giving to others and most of all she has supported my dreams, even when they didn't seem to make sense.

Throughout my career, I have been blessed to have colleagues and friends who have shared their knowledge and insights, and who have challenged me to grow. I would like to express my gratitude to each and every one of them for their unwavering support and guidance.

To my friends, who have been there for me through thick and thin, I want to express my deepest gratitude. Your unwavering belief in me and your constant words of encouragement have been a driving force behind my journey as an author. Your honest feedback and constructive criticism have helped shape this book into its final form.

I would also like to acknowledge the support of all the Black people who participated in the Experience Chasm Survey and interviews that informed some of the content of this book. Their willingness to share their stories and insights has added depth and richness to the narrative. I am humbled by their openness and grateful for their contribution to this project.

My sincere appreciation goes to the editorial team at Bloomsbury Business for their meticulous attention to detail and their commitment to producing a high-quality book. Their expertise and professionalism have been instrumental in bringing this project to fruition.

Lastly, I want to acknowledge my husband and kids for their unwavering love and support throughout this journey. They have been my pillar of strength, providing the emotional support and understanding that I needed during the highs and lows of writing this book. Their belief in me, even when I doubted myself, has been invaluable.

Writing this book has been a labour of love, and I am immensely grateful to everyone who has played a part in its creation. Without their support, encouragement, and inspiration, this endeavour would not have been possible.

My heartfelt thanks go out to each and every individual who has been a part of this journey, whether big or small. Together, we have made this dream a reality.

Index